AMPHIBIANS
OF EUROPE, NORTH AFRICA & THE MIDDLE EAST
A PHOTOGRAPHIC GUIDE

Christophe Dufresnes

AMPHIBIANS
OF EUROPE, NORTH AFRICA
& THE MIDDLE EAST
A PHOTOGRAPHIC GUIDE

Christophe Dufresnes

BLOOMSBURY WILDLIFE

LONDON • OXFORD • NEW YORK • NEW DELHI • SYDNEY

To my little froglet, Chloé

BLOOMSBURY WILDLIFE
Bloomsbury Publishing Plc
50 Bedford Square, London, WC1B 3DP, UK

BLOOMSBURY, BLOOMSBURY WILDLIFE and the Diana logo are trademarks of
Bloomsbury Publishing Plc

First published in the United Kingdom, 2019

A catalogue record for this book is available from the British Library

Library of Congress Cataloguing-in-Publication data has been applied for

ISBN: PB: 978-1-4729-4137-4; ePDF: 978-1-4729-4138-1; ePub: 978-1-4729-4139-8

2 4 6 8 10 9 7 5 3 1

Designed by Rod Teasdale
Printed and bound in China by RR Donnelley

To find out more about our authors and books visit www.bloomsbury.com
and sign up for our newsletters

Contents

Foreword

My earliest memories as a child living in the countryside are of tadpoles dwelling in the fountain in our garden, choruses of tree frogs in nearby ponds, and the aquatic parade of Alpine Newts, a paradigm of grace and elegance. These early aesthetic experiences largely contributed to my decision to become a zoologist.

Amphibians have been around for a very long time. They were the first tetrapods on Earth, having evolved from lungfish in the late Devonian. Although the so-called great age of amphibians has long passed, they still outnumber mammals in terms of species richness, with close to 7,000 described to date. And this number continues to grow – more than 30 new species were described in 2017 in the Peruvian Amazon alone, along with a similar number in the forests of Madagascar.

Ranging in size from just 7mm in the case of *Paedophryne amauensis* (the smallest known vertebrate, from New Guinea) to 1.8m for the Chinese Giant Salamander (*Andrias davidianus*), amphibians have a fascinating life cycle, characterised by a rapid and complete metamorphosis between the aquatic larval stage and the terrestrial adult stage – reminiscent of the great leap forward accomplished when vertebrates first colonised terrestrial habitats. This complex life cycle demands specific ecological requirements, which for the most part constrain their distribution to moist habitats. This explains why many species are limited to tropical rainforests (today the most rapidly disappearing biome). As the present book shows, however, Europe's 137 native amphibian species are also remarkably diverse. They display an impressive array of physiological adaptations to a range of habitats, from desert landscapes to high mountains, and to a variety of life cycles, from the paternal care of midwife toads to the viviparous habits and move away from water seen in Alpine Salamanders.

Being ancient, however, is no guarantee an animal will be perennial. Since the late 1980s, amphibian populations have been subject to dramatic declines and local extinctions worldwide. Although the ongoing sixth global extinction is affecting all living beings, the decline in amphibians is certainly one of the most critical, partly due to their complex reproductive needs and permeable skins. Many causes have been pinpointed, including habitat destruction, the rise in pollutants (including endocrine disruptors) and diseases such as chytridiomycosis. Around half of the described amphibian species are declining, and a third are already threatened with extinction. Europe is directly concerned: habitat destruction, pollutants and disease might drive more than half of our amphibian fauna to extinction within 40 years.

I strongly believe that field guides like this one by Christophe Dufresnes contribute directly to limiting the erosion of biodiversity, by drawing the attention of our fellow citizens to the beauty and fragility of nature. Christophe is not only a first-class scientist who has contributed significantly to our knowledge of amphibian systematics and phylogeography throughout Europe, but is also an excellent field naturalist with wide-ranging interests. This guide, which contains an exhaustive description of all Western Palearctic amphibian species, will be an irreplaceable field companion for naturalists, thanks to its high-quality photographs, named and illustrated key identification features, concise and informative species descriptions, habitat and ecological information, and up-to-date distribution maps. Not least, it will help to preserve amphibians as a crucial component of our European fauna, so that this living heritage can be passed down to our children and grandchildren.

Nicolas Perrin, Switzerland, January 2019

Introduction

Most people have seen a frog hopping across the road on a rainy night, and many of us may have raised tadpoles as a child, been frightened by weird croaking sounds at night or even wondered whether salamanders can actually survive wood fires, as the stories claim. Amphibians are everywhere: in domestic gardens, along forest hiking trails, in the streams you fill your flask from, in the trough your neighbour's cow drinks from and beneath the snow you ski on. Yet only keen enthusiasts will be able to experience their wide diversity in its entirety. Those who go out into the remote countryside after the sun has gone down, equipped with only a headlamp and a pair of boots but driven by a thirst for nocturnal wetland adventures, will be rewarded with an answer to that existential question: how can such a racket be caused by such a cute little creature?

This book aims at provoking that thirst for amphibian adventures. It reveals how to discover those spectacular frogs, toads, salamanders and newts that live just beyond our front door or on the other side of our continent, and provides useful information for their straightforward identification. As readers will discover, not all frogs are green and they do not all look the same!

Amphibian Evolution

The term 'amphibian' is the combination of the ancient Greek words *amphi*, meaning 'both kinds', and *bios*, meaning 'life', and conveys the animals' dual lifestyles, on land and in water. Amphibians are the oldest tetrapods, or animals with four limbs. They evolved during the Devonian period, around 370 million years ago, from fish that had primitive lungs and bony fins with digits, enabling them to live temporarily out of water. Over the following millions of years, they developed adaptations such as more efficient lungs, nostrils, thicker skin, ears, and a morphology better suited to terrestrial locomotion and feeding, which allowed them to survive for longer periods on dry land. Vertebrate life was essentially aquatic during the Devonian, and the land was mostly inhabited by plants and insects. Hence, during the following Carboniferous and Permian periods (360–250 million years ago), early amphibians diversified and occupied the top of the terrestrial food chain. Some species reached enormous sizes, comparable to modern crocodiles; these included *Prionosuchus* species, the largest amphibians that ever existed, measuring up to 9m in length.

This amphibian dominance was abruptly stopped by the most severe mass extinction event known on Earth, the Great Dying, which took place at the end of the Permian period around 252 million years ago, during which up to 96 per cent of marine species and 70 per cent of terrestrial vertebrates became extinct. Subsequently, the remaining amphibians were outcompeted by reptiles – notably the dinosaurs – and their size and diversity decreased. This period was also the trigger for the split and evolution of the only amphibian lineage that has survived into the modern era: the subclass Lissamphibia, which includes the three extant amphibian groups.

Amphibian Classification

The first of the three living amphibian groups is the clade Salientia (from the Latin word meaning 'to jump'), which includes some extinct proto-frogs and members of the order Anura, the modern frogs and toads. Anurans usually have long hindlimbs and are tailless (*anura* is Greek for 'without tail'). They are found on every continent except Antarctica, although most occur in the tropics, and are by far the most diverse group, with around 4,800 species out of the 7,000 or so amphibians recorded to date. The smallest living vertebrate is a 7mm-long microhylid frog from Papua New Guinea, *Paedophryne amauensis*. Three anuran suborders are broadly accepted: the primitive Archaeobatrachia, including the two European families Alytidae and Bombinatoridae; the less primitive Mesobatrachia, also including two European families, Pelobatidae and

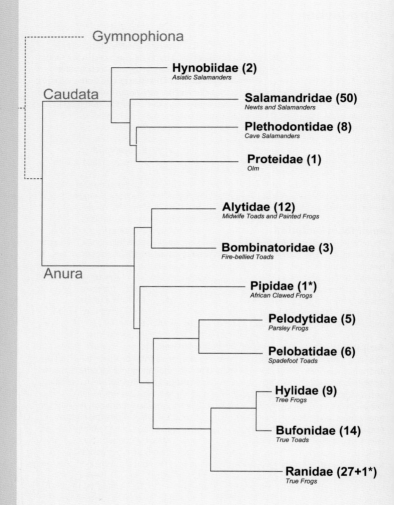

Fig 1 Phylogeny of the amphibian families found in the Western Palearctic (in bold). The number of species present in this ecozone are indicated in parentheses after each family.

* exotic species

Pelodytidae; and Neobatrachia, the 'modern frogs', including the vast majority (96 per cent) of living anurans.

The second group of amphibians is the order Caudata (or Urodela), which contains all salamanders. These possess an elongated lizard-like body, ending in a tail (*cauda* means 'tail' in Latin). Commonly known as urodeles, they may be purely terrestrial or purely aquatic, but many species spend time in both habitats. Their size ranges from the largest living amphibian, the Chinese Giant Salamander (*Andrias davidianus*), measuring up to 1.8m, to the miniature Veracruz Pigmy Salamander (*Thorius pennatulus*) from Mexico, at just 2cm in length. Caudata are mostly distributed in the northern hemisphere and are further subdivided into three suborders: the primitive Cryptobranchoidea, with three relict species of giant salamanders in Asia and North America; Sirenoidea, with four extant species of eel-like aquatic salamanders; and Salamandroidea, which contains all the remaining salamanders, including the semi-aquatic species from the subfamily Pleurodelinae, commonly referred to as newts.

The third amphibian group is the order Gymnophiona (or Apoda), commonly known as caecilians and comprising worm-like creatures inhabiting the tropical regions of Africa, Asia and America. Caecilians are limbless and spend much of their life underground, in damp soil and associated vegetation debris. They are usually small in size (5–15cm), although some species are exceptions to this general rule – including the Colombian Thompson's Caecilian (*Caecilia thompsoni*), which grows to more than a metre in length. The group remains poorly known, and, to this day, only about 160 species from six families have been described.

Contrary to popular belief and some superficial similarities, amphibians are not related to reptiles. Yet both are often considered together, notably under the general term 'herpetology'. This habit dates back to early classifications made by the pioneering naturalist Carl Linnaeus in the eighteenth century, who grouped amphibians and reptiles into a single clade, and it has persisted despite taxonomic irrelevance.

Amphibian Diversity in the Western Palearctic

The Western Palearctic spans the entire European continent, along with North Africa and the Middle East. Altogether, this area forms an independent biogeographic region isolated by the Arctic ice cap to the north, the Atlantic Ocean to the west, the Saharan and Middle Eastern deserts to the south and south-east, and the Ural Mountains to the north-east. Its heterogeneity offers diverse environments – from hot, dry deserts and Mediterranean shrublands, to temperate forests and alpine meadows – that are inhabited by equally diverse amphibians. Some are specialists, like the brook newts *Euproctus* and *Calotriton*, which are confined to mountains streams, or the parsley frogs (Pelodytidae), which live in dry Mediterranean meadows. Others are generalists and are found in several types of environments, from deserts to mountaintops, like brown frogs (*Rana*), water frogs (*Pelophylax*) and *Bufo* toads.

Many amphibian groups diversified across the Western Palearctic over the last few million years, as a result of geological and climatic events. One of the most remarkable of these episodes was the Messinian salinity crisis some 6 million years ago, when the Strait of Gibraltar was sealed off and the Mediterranean Sea subsequently evaporated, connecting islands to the mainland. When the strait reopened, 5.3 million years ago, the Atlantic refilled the Mediterranean Basin, cutting off amphibian populations in North Africa and on islands like Corsica, Sardinia, Crete and Cyprus. These isolated groups subsequently evolved as different species.

Another major driver of amphibian diversity was the Pleistocene ice ages. As the orbital cycles of our planet fluctuated, the distance between the Earth and the Sun varied and the climate of the northern hemisphere alternated between dry, cold glacial periods (i.e. the ice ages) and mild interglacials. The last ice age endured for about 100,000 years and reached its peak some 21,000 years ago at the Last Glacial Maximum, after which the climate rapidly warmed to the conditions we experience today. These changes profoundly affected the distribution of wildlife: during the glacial periods, northern areas such as the UK and Fennoscandia were covered with ice, and others like northern France, Germany and Poland featured tundra deserts, both unsuitable for ectothermic species like amphibians, dependent on external heat sources for body warmth. As a consequence, in many amphibians the only Palearctic populations that persisted through the ice ages were restricted to southern regions such as the Iberian, Apennine and Balkan peninsulas, as well as the Black Sea and Caspian Sea coasts. These glacial refugia sheltered populations but kept them isolated from one another over millions of years, and they progressively evolved into distinct species. During interglacials, such as the one we are in now, some of these species expanded northward; today, they meet in what biogeographers call 'secondary contact zones', where they eventually hybridise.

At a regional scale, the diversity of amphibians in the Western Palearctic was further shaped by local environmental barriers. In particular, the Iberian, Apennine and Balkan peninsulas are topographically complex, and so different lineages have evolved within them. In peninsular Italy, for example, the Apennine Mountains have acted as a barrier between its northern and southern populations (e.g. of *Salamandrina*), leading to diversification. In Iberia, aridity has prevented amphibian populations from persisting beyond the coasts, and several frogs (e.g. *Pelodytes* and *Alytes*) have evolved distinct species or subspecies in Portugal and northern Spain (Atlantic coast), and south-eastern Spain (Mediterranean coast). The Balkans offer several microrefugia (e.g. the Adriatic and Hellenic coasts, and the Pannonian Basin), which again have resulted in different evolutionary lineages (e.g. in *Lissotriton* and *Triturus*). In North Africa, the Algerian

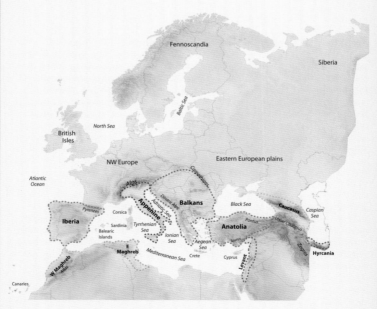

Fig 2 The Western Palearctic and its major biogeographic regions. The main continental areas where amphibians persisted and diversified throughout the Quaternary ice ages are indicated by coloured outlines.

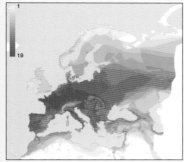 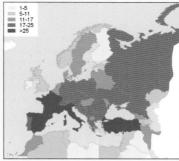

Fig 3 Amphibian diversity across the Western Palearctic. Left: the number of species by 20x20km cells. Right: the number of species by country. The diversity hotspots correspond to the main biogeographic regions (see Fig 2) but also the areas of post-glacial secondary contacts, such as north-west Europe.

Desert has isolated species in Morocco and Tunisia from one another (e.g. *Discoglossus*, *Pelophylax* and *Pleurodeles*). Across the Middle East, multiple divergences were caused by desertification and the uplift of the Anatolian Diagonal (e.g. *Pelophylax*, *Rana*, *Triturus* and *Ommatotriton*).

The ecological tolerance and dispersal capacity of a species relate directly to its ability to overcome environmental barriers. Consequently, specialist amphibians with low dispersal capabilities have diversified more than those that are readily able to disperse. An extreme case is the Lycian salamanders (*Lyciasalamandra*), which are restricted to single valleys in south-western Anatolia and have evolved into multiple species only tens of kilometres from each other. The same is true for the cave salamanders (*Speleomantes*), where different species within the genus share adjacent hills throughout Sardinia. In contrast, some single species with broad ecological tolerances – including the Common Toad (page 19), European Tree Frog (page 61) and European Pool Frog (page 100) – have spread thousands of kilometres across Europe since the end of the last ice age.

Today, regions with the highest amphibian diversity are located at intermediate latitudes, where species that survived the last ice age in different glacial refugia have since met in secondary contact zones. Ancient and modern human civilisations have also affected the distribution of some amphibians: several species were brought to islands naturally deprived of them, like the Canaries and Balearics, while others were translocated throughout Europe as part of trading exchanges. Endemism, where a species is found in only one place and nowhere else, is seen in southern regions and offshore islands in the Western Palearctic, where amphibian species remained isolated.

Together, these conditions and processes have influenced modern patterns of amphibian diversity in the Western Palearctic. This book examines the resulting 139 species and their subspecies, a list that accounts for the latest evolutionary genetics research on amphibians. Many closely related species are cryptic, meaning that they look very similar and can be distinguished only by genetics and geographic distribution.

The use of molecular tools has revolutionised our perception of amphibian diversity and many new species have consequently been discovered over the past 20 years. But if two amphibians look alike, what makes them different species? The formal definition of a species is that it is a biological entity that is reproductively isolated. While this is straightforward when applied to distant taxa, it becomes tricky when two species hybridise and reproductive isolation between them is therefore only partial. It is even trickier when diverged lineages do not have the chance to hybridise because they inhabit different geographic regions. Therefore, defining a 'species' is somewhat subjective, and the taxonomic position of many amphibians remains controversial among specialists. The same is true for subspecies described on the basis of morphological or colour characteristics, but lacking any meaningful genetic identity. The species and subspecies named as such in this book reflect an evolutionary biologist's opinion, and include the taxa that have been formally described and confirmed by molecular analyses to the best current knowledge.

The Amphibian Life Cycle

Unlike the other tetrapod classes (reptiles, birds and mammals), amphibians are not amniotes: their eggs lack impervious membranes and they require water for reproduction. Some salamanders are an exception, bypassing this stage by giving birth to fully formed young (e.g. alpine salamanders) or by keeping their eggs in humid areas (e.g. the cave salamanders).

Most European amphibians are both terrestrial and aquatic, and reproduction is seasonal. At temperate latitudes, they spend summer and autumn on the ground, hunting invertebrates such as worms, spiders and insects. In winter, they hibernate in burrows, tree or rock cavities, or simply in the humid soil, during which their metabolism is highly reduced. When the light cycle and temperature increase in spring, they come out of hibernation and reproduce. At Mediterranean latitudes, this dynamic is inverted: amphibians are mainly active during autumn and winter, and aestivate (go through a period of inactivity) during the dry summer.

Many species have nocturnal habits, especially during reproduction, a strategy that

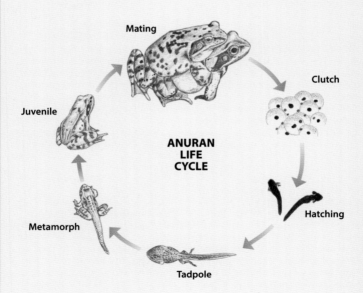

Fig 4 The life cycle of anurans (frogs and toads). Timing of mating, as well as duration of each developmental stage, varies between and within species, since it largely depends on environmental conditions such as temperature.

Adult anatomy

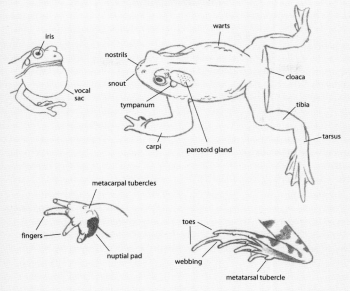

Tadpole anatomy

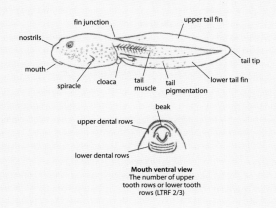

Mouth ventral view
The number of upper
tooth rows or lower tooth
rows (LTRF 2/3)

Fig 5 Many of the main anatomical features of anurans are important for species identification.

probably evolved to avoid predation. During the day, some roost on vegetation (e.g. tree frogs), in ground litter (e.g. brown frogs), under rocks (e.g. toads and salamanders) or directly in water (e.g. newts and water frogs). Their peak of activity is usually at dusk, when it is dark but the air and water remain warm and invertebrates are still on the go.

Amphibians breed in varying types of water bodies, from temporary puddles left by forestry trucks to large wetlands in river deltas. These are usually located near meadows or forests, where the animals spend the rest of the year. Rain showers are the main cues for the start of the breeding season: not only do they fill the ponds required for reproduction, but the resulting humidity promotes amphibian movement on the ground. Adults then leave their winter quarters and travel towards breeding sites, a journey known as amphibian migration and one that covers distances ranging from tens of metres to several kilometres. Many species are capable of navigating their way via complex mechanisms (e.g. using the stars), and they often display homing behaviour, finding their way back to the same site year after year.

Reproduction in Anura

Amphibian reproduction involves both simple and complex courtship behaviours. Anurans reproduce in so-called 'leks', where males gather together in groups at breeding sites and call in chorus to attract females. Calls differ greatly between anuran groups, and include rattles, rumbles, croaks and whistles, all of which can sometimes be confused with the sounds made by other animals. In anurans, they are used for species recognition and some choruses may be heard many kilometres away.

Once the females reach a lek, it is not clear how they select males or if calls convey information regarding the quality of individuals. One plausible theory is that females actually choose at random, mating with the first male they reach. If this is the case, males in better condition – which are more often present at the lek over the season, because they don't need to leave as often to forage for food – will have better odds of mating than weaker males, which need to forage more frequently. In some species like Common Toads, females do not get to choose and males force mating aggressively; on occasion, several males mate with one female simultaneously, which may result in the death of the female.

In anurans, mating involves a position called amplexus. In this, the male clasps the female on her back, either at the armpits (called axillary amplexus, and seen in Hylidae, Bufonidae and Ranidae), or at the waist (called lumbar amplexus, and seen in other Western Palearctic families). He stays on her as she searches for a good spawning site, and externally fertilises the eggs as she lays them, usually on or around aquatic vegetation, or simply in the water or on the pond floor. Clutch sizes vary from tens of eggs to thousands, arranged in gelatinous networks that form 'grapes' (in frogs) or 'strings' (in toads). Amplexus usually lasts a few hours, but it can be extended over several days, especially if it was formed far away from the breeding site. The couple detaches after spawning.

Anuran tadpoles and metamorphosis

Several days after spawning (the exact time depends on water temperature and species), anuran eggs hatch into wholly aquatic larvae, known as tadpoles. Tadpoles have a globular body and a compressed tail that is used for swimming. They breathe through internal or external gills and are usually herbivorous, although they can also feed on carrion (notably other tadpoles). As they mature – a process that lasts from several weeks to several years, depending on the species and environmental conditions – they undergo metamorphosis, during which their body changes physically towards the adult form. They grow limbs (the hindlimbs first, then the forelimbs), develop lungs, and rearrange their mouth and organs to transit towards a carnivorous adult lifestyle. The size of tadpoles varies greatly between species and the stage of development. Usually measuring a few millimetres on hatching, they can grow dramatically, reaching lengths of up to 25cm in the South American *Pseudis* frogs, but more usually around

3–15cm in European species. They later shrink in size as they progressively metamorph.

In most Western Palearctic anurans, metamorphosis takes place in summer. The juvenile frogs and toads then hunt near their birthplace before overwintering. Reaching full adulthood may take several years depending on food availability and the length of the active period, and in the meantime, individuals are considered subadults. Males usually reach sexual maturity before females, and individuals keep growing in size as they age. In the wild, the lifespan of anurans is around 5–10 years, but it can be as much as 30 years if populations are not exposed to any particular risks and if their annual period of activity is short.

Reproduction in Caudata

Reproductive behaviour in Caudata is quite different. Instead of using vocalisation, newts and salamanders rely on olfactory and tactile cues to identify and select mates. Before the breeding season, newts change their skin: they have a terrestrial phase in autumn and winter, when they superficially resemble salamanders, but switch to an aquatic phase on entering the water in early spring. This moulting produces the impressive dorsal crest of males, as well as a developed tail fin that is adapted to their essentially aquatic lifestyle during the breeding season.

Male newts are territorial and try to occupy the best spots of the pond, where there is suitable vegetation for spawning. They display elaborate courtship behaviours to seduce females. When a female encounters a male, he will 'dance' in front of her, waving and whipping his tail while excreting pheromones. If she is seduced, he will release his sperm into the water in the form of a gelatinous bag called a spermatophore, which she absorbs with her cloaca so that her eggs can be fertilised internally. Some species that breed in streams have evolved physical contact, enabling cloaca-to-cloaca spermatophore transfer,

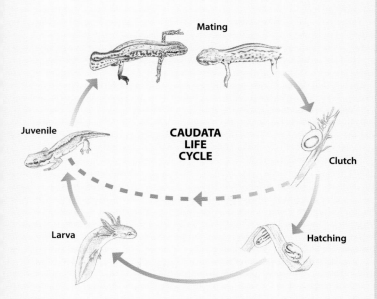

Fig 6 The life cycle of Caudata (newts and salamanders). Some species bypass the egg or even larval stages, and give birth to larvae (larviparous species) or fully-formed juveniles (viviparous) respectively.

Adult anatomy

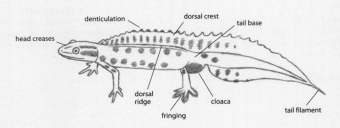

Larval anatomy

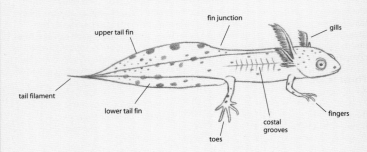

Fig 7 Many of the main anatomical features of Caudata are important for species identification.

in order to prevent the spermatophore being washed away by the current. Unlike the eggs of frogs and toads, newt eggs are attached individually to vegetation or rocks, and females produce a maximum of a few hundred eggs.

In contrast with newts, salamanders typically mate on land. As in anurans, they perform amplexus, although in salamanders this is ventral, with the male positioning himself under the female. After he emits pheromones, the male deposits his spermatophore on the ground and the female picks it up with her vent. Many species (e.g. Common Fire Salamander; page 161) are larviparous, with the eggs developing internally and females giving birth to aquatic larvae; some (e.g. Alpine Salamander; page 164, and Lycian salamanders) are viviparous, giving birth to fully formed juveniles; and some (e.g. cave salamanders) produce terrestrial eggs that hatch directly into juveniles, without a larval stage.

Caudata larvae and metamorphosis

All Caudata larvae are recognisable by their three pairs of external gills. The larvae of pond species usually have broad tail fins and well-developed feathery gills, while stream larvae are usually slender with short gills. All are carnivorous, preying on small aquatic animals like insects and anuran tadpoles. At metamorphosis, the larvae develop limbs, eyelids, a tongue and teeth, and lose their gills and tail fins. Some, however, are neotenic (or paedomorphic): they do not metamorphose and keep larval traits (e.g. gills) during their adult life, as in the Mexican Axolotl (*Ambystoma mexicanum*). In Europe, only the Olm (page 188) is purely neotenic, although occasional individual cases of neoteny are reported in many species, such as the Smooth Newt (page 122) and Alpine Newt.

Caudata reach sexual maturity after several years and live about 10–20 years – and potentially much longer. The Olm has a human-like lifespan: it reproduces after 15 years and then every 12 years, and lives up to a century.

Amphibian defence
The remarkable longevity of amphibians given their relatively small size is due both to their long seasonal periods of inactivity (hibernation) and to their various defence mechanisms. Many species of toads and salamanders are poisonous and have few predators. Some advertise this toxicity by vivid colours (e.g. *Salamandra*), a feature called aposematism. Others bear cryptic colours for camouflage, mimicking the hues of their main environment (e.g. the leafy green of the *Hyla* tree frogs, or the dead-leaf brown of the forest *Rana* frogs) and undergoing physiological colour changes, like chameleons. Some combine both strategies (e.g. *Bombina* toads), being dull on their back but colourful on their belly, and exhibiting the latter only in the face of immediate danger, in a flexible torsion known as the unken reflex. Finally, some salamanders use tail autotomy to distract and escape predators: like lizards, they lose their tail, which then wriggles for a moment as a form of decoy. The tail regrows over time. Salamanders are capable of regenerating different kinds of tissues, and even complex body parts such as the eyes.

Threats and Conservation
Amphibians are among the most endangered animals worldwide. About half of the 7,000 or so known species are declining, and a third are in danger of extinction. In the Western Palearctic, 56 out of 111 species that have been properly assessed are threatened or near threatened on a global scale, and almost all are decreasing in number over at least some parts of their range.

In Europe, the primary cause of this decline is the destruction of habitats. Amphibians rely on both terrestrial and aquatic habitats to fulfil their life cycle. Human exploitation of land has resulted in the loss of meadows, forests and especially wetlands, and thus the direct disappearance of their associated species. As the landscape becomes fragmented, populations inhabiting the remaining patches of suitable habitat become isolated and face serious risks since local declines cannot be compensated for by immigration. Population disconnection can further trigger genetic inbreeding, with individuals having no choice other than to mate with relatives. The subsequent decrease of genetic diversity impedes the potential of individuals to cope with environmental changes. Fragmentation between wintering and breeding sites is also a threat. In particular, roads acting as barriers between the two represent a huge danger, as amphibians are frequently killed by vehicles during their migration.

The alteration of habitats – for instance, due to the intensification of grazing by livestock – and the pollution of surface water by chemical contaminants are also serious problems. Pesticides and heavy metals, used in intensive agriculture practices, are known to increase larval mortality and induce developmental deformities. Moreover, pesticides – including the widely used atrazine – are endocrine disruptors, interfering with the hormonal signalling that is necessary for proper sexual development and reproductive behaviour in amphibians, thereby inducing sterility, demasculinisation and hermaphroditism. Crop fertilisers, which pollute the water systems with different forms of nitrogen, also alter the feeding activity, development and survival of amphibians.

Amphibians are ectothermic and as such are susceptible to changes in temperature and humidity. Global warming will ultimately affect species distributions, inducing altitudinal and latitudinal shifts. This will have a particular impact on species that do not move much (i.e. have low dispersal capabilities) and/or that simply have nowhere else to go (i.e. have a restricted range). Global warming will also have a direct negative impact on the availability of water, an effect that is already palpable in some Mediterranean regions. Many amphibians breed in temporary ponds that progressively dry out during spring and summer, and early desiccation means the death of all larvae that have not had time to reach metamorphosis. Breeding phenology may also be affected: amphibians exit hibernation and start reproducing following environmental cues such as changes in temperature and moisture. Many species are now breeding earlier and earlier every year, in turn becoming more vulnerable to the freezing episodes that are common at the beginning of the season. Episodic warm periods can also promote pathogen growth and disease outbreaks. Finally, European amphibians are susceptible to ultraviolet B radiation, levels of which have increased following the destruction of stratospheric ozone.

A widely reported amphibian threat is chytridiomycosis, an infectious disease caused by the fungal pathogens *Batrachochytrium dendrobatidis* and *B. salamandrivorans*. These agents have been responsible for catastrophic declines in hundreds of species, and are now present on every continent. They infect the keratin layers of the outer skin of adults, as well as the mouthparts of tadpoles, thickening their tissues and hence inhibiting breathing, hydration and thermoregulation, eventually resulting in death. Some species appear resistant, but they may still act as vectors of the disease. In Europe, outbreaks were confirmed in several western countries in the 2000s, most of them introduced with the invasive American Bullfrog (page 116).

Other amphibian pathogens include viruses in the genus *Ranavirus*, which cause systematic diseases and have been associated with mass declines. Many species may also exhibit red-leg syndrome (reddening of the underparts), indicative of septicaemia caused by a bacterium (often *Aeromonas hydrophila*) and responsible for some population die-offs. Parasitic fungi (e.g. *Saprolegnia*) are another threat, infecting eggs and larvae, with lethal effects.

Overharvesting can have adverse effects on amphibian populations. Frogs' legs feature

Above Amphibians are at risk of contracting many diseases, some of which are the result of human activities. Here this poor Common Toad is infected by a flesh-eating fly (*Lucilia bufonivora*) whose larvae live in the toad's nasal cavity.

Above Water pollution is a major issue for the conservation of amphibians. Pesticides, fertilisers and litter are all threats to freshwater wildlife.

in the cuisine of several cultures and appear on the menus of many restaurants worldwide. As a result, exploited wild populations are facing pressure, sometimes leading to declines. While the main exporting countries are in Asia and South America, Turkey remains a major provider of *Pelophylax* water frogs. Overcollection for the pet trade is another concern, especially of newts and salamanders, which are popular in terrariums but may be rare and localised in the wild (e.g. *Neurergus*). Furthermore, amphibian trade may also result in the unwanted release of imported species outside their native range, and the consequent risk of biological invasions.

Non-native animals introduced by humans can pose a serious danger to native amphibians. Some of these alien species have become invasive, increasing in number and disrupting ecosystem dynamics. In the Western Palearctic, introduced fish like the Rainbow Trout (*Oncorhynchus mykiss*) and mosquitofish (*Gambusia*) (released for recreational fishing and mosquito control respectively) prey on eggs and larvae, and are involved in the decline of several frogs. On a local scale, people often systematically introduce goldfish to ornamental ponds, threatening local amphibians and/or preventing their colonisation from nearby sites. The introduction of the Signal Crayfish (*Pacifastacus leniusculus*) has had similar consequences: imported from North America to Europe in the 1960s, it has since spread throughout the continent. On land, introduced Raccoons (*Procyon lotor*) predate adult frogs and salamanders, especially in the Caucasus.

Sometimes, however, the worst enemies of amphibians are other amphibians. In Europe, exotic American Bullfrogs and African Clawed Frogs (page 117) are spreading from their initial release sites, threatening local species through competition, predation and the transmission of diseases. Yet the most frequent translocations are of species within Europe, following historical imports for frogs' legs and releases by amphibian enthusiasts. For instance, several Italian species – including the Italian Pool Frog (page 101) and Italian Crested Newt (page 134) – are now widely found north of the Alps. Beyond the ecological issues, these species can also compromise native close relatives through hybridisation.

Above African Clawed Frogs were imported to Europe from South Africa for research and pharmaceutical purposes. They brought with them the terrible chytrid fungus – for which they are asymptomatic – that threatens many species around the world.

As we have seen, the vast majority of the threats faced by amphibians are a direct consequence of human activities such as urbanisation, intensification of agriculture and international trade. As expected, the well-developed north-western European countries are the main culprits in the Western Palearctic, with many species appearing on their national Red Lists. In contrast, the same species are less threatened in southern countries, which have retained more traditional farming practices. Southern amphibian populations also usually display a higher genetic diversity, as they remained stable throughout the Pleistocene ice ages. This diversity may allow them to adapt to current changing environments and global warming, and it is therefore crucial to preserve these populations. To this end, all amphibians are now protected in most European countries and anyone capturing them needs permission to do so.

Protecting amphibians is challenging because of the need to consider both aquatic and terrestrial habitats, as well as the connectivity between them. As they are sensitive to a wide array of threats, amphibians are environmental indicators: their presence is often a sign of healthy ecosystems in unpolluted habitats. Nature reserves with networks of ponds and wetlands offer sanctuaries, and remain the only sure way to protect amphibian communities. In these areas and others, the impact of car traffic can be limited by specific driving restrictions or infrastructures such as fauna tunnels.

Preventing the spread of diseases and invasive species is everyone's responsibility, from private pond owners to professional biologists. Amphibians should not be transported between different regions or even different sites in the same region, and the release of fish or crayfish (for ornament or fishing) must be avoided at all costs. Moreover, fighting chytridiomycosis necessitates the cleaning of equipment (notably boots) with multi-purpose disinfectants between different sites.

Legislation to reduce other types of threats – such as the international trade in amphibians, and pesticide and fertiliser use – is being improved but it remains difficult to enforce. The preservation of our natural landscapes will obviously be dependent on future environmental policies at both the regional and global scale. In the meantime, educating the general public about amphibians and their ecosystems is one of our best hopes for securing the future of these fascinating animals.

How to Use This Book

This book packages up relevant species information into compact yet comprehensive single-page layouts, facilitating immediate access for readers. Species are arranged by families, with similar taxa featured consecutively for easy comparison. The species-rich family Salamandridae is further split into six distinct groups of closely related taxa.

Each family or group is introduced with an opener that provides general information on the main characteristics and diversity of the member species, both worldwide and in the Western Palearctic. Species are listed in the form of a phylogenetic tree – a 'species genealogy' based on molecular sequences – giving an idea of how they evolved and which show the greatest differentiation.

The individual species accounts are divided in three parts: photographs, with numbered identification criteria pointed out; interesting facts about the species; and key information relating to the species, including a distribution map, the list of identification criteria, the usual size range, a description of the habitat, the usual breeding period, a description of any sexual dimorphism, a transcription of breeding calls (for anurans), a description of the egg clutch, a description of the tadpole or larvae, a note of the number of subspecies (if any), and the status of the species according to the International Union for Conservation of Nature Red List of Threatened Species (IUCN Red List). Each of these key areas is explained in more detail below.

Photographs The photos included in the accounts are intended to show useful criteria for a species-level field identification while also portraying how attractive amphibians can be. All the images were taken by informed naturalists and/or professional biologists who provided sound information regarding the taxonomy and location of the species shown. Smaller photos illustrate specific behaviour or other features such as habitats or larvae.

Distribution maps The maps of species distribution have been created using information from the IUCN Red List (www.iucnredlist.org), adjusted as necessary using complementary reports (i.e. scientific publications and regional atlases), accounting for taxonomic advances. Note that the margins of many species are still not clear (especially for parapatric species, which eventually hybridise), and observations made at the periphery of the illustrated ranges should not necessarily be discarded. Localised populations, as for the case of introductions, are noted with a star.

Identification criteria This section provides a list of the key features the reader may focus on in the field to help identify a species, arranged by relevance. Where applicable, the key features are shown in the accompanying image(s). Note that many closely related species are cryptic, meaning that they look very similar, and that geographic location is then necessary for determination. The general characteristics shared by several cryptic species appear in the account of the nominal species, and differences between the named species and the nominal species are then mentioned in the individual accounts. When confusion with other sympatric species is possible, specific comparative criteria are reported. Figs 5 and 7 illustrate and name some of the body parts mentioned in the species accounts.

Size The usual size range of adults, considering both sexes together, is given in centimetres. Note that specimens smaller than the indicated size (juveniles) may be found. For species where many age classes coexist, only a maximum size is given because a range would be misleading.

Habitat The section relating to habitat briefly describes the type of environment – and especially the type of water body – where the species can be observed. Since many species can be easily seen only while breeding, the characteristics of breeding sites are highlighted.

Reproductive period This section details the time of the year during which the species usually breeds and can be more easily observed. This varies with latitude and altitude: southern and lowland populations reproduce earlier than northern and mountain populations. As such, wide time spans are often reported for widespread species, even when the actual breeding window of their population is short. Note that breeding may also be observed outside the described reproductive period, especially for Mediterranean species. Tadpole identification can also be aided by taking note of the reproductive period – their presumed laying date can be compared with the reproductive periods of the potential species.

Sexual dimorphism A short description is given of any noticeable differences between adult males and females. Some of these are displayed during the breeding period only.

Calls A written transcription of the mating call of anuran species is provided, with a description of associated features such as behaviour and context. While every effort has been made to render wildlife sounds as letters accurately, these transcriptions obviously remain partially subjective and are bound to vary according to the voice and accent of the reader. Hence, they should not be relied upon alone for species identification, but instead used to confirm a suspicion regarding a species that can be physically observed. Moreover, note that amphibians may sometimes sporadically exhibit different non-mating sounds, such as territorial or release calls.

Spawn The description of egg clutches includes useful information such as the number of eggs, their size and colours, how they are arranged and the substrate on which they are deposited.

Tadpoles/larvae A list of the main characteristics of the tadpole (Anura) or larvae (Caudata) is provided, including its size, colour, position of the cloaca and spiracle, and the form of the caudal fins. Figs 5 and 7 illustrate and name the body parts mentioned in the species accounts. Specific behavioural features are also reported. Instead of giving a long, complex identification key, these short descriptions (in some cases complemented by photos) allow readers to discriminate rapidly between the young of a few candidate species at any one time and place.

Subspecies Where relevant, the number of subspecies is given, along with a cross reference to the appendix where further details can be found (photos and distributions). The validity of many subspecies is currently doubtful, and this book takes into account the latest scientific studies, notably molecular evidence.

IUCN Red List This section lists the level of threat faced by the species at the global scale, as evaluated by the International Union for the Conservation of Nature (IUCN). Relatively safe species qualify as Least Concern or Near Threatened, whereas threatened species may be classed as Vulnerable, Endangered or Critically Endangered. These status classifications are determined using multiple criteria related to the species' population demography, rates of decline, extent of distribution range and potential threats. Note that while widespread species are often classed as Least Concern thanks to their current large distribution ranges, at the regional scale many of their populations actually face a precarious situation. Finally, many Western Palearctic amphibians have yet to be evaluated by the IUCN owing to recent taxonomic revisions or incomplete monitoring data.

Glossary

Aestivation The rest period undertaken by some amphibians in the Mediterranean summer, when conditions are too dry and hot for any activity. Aestivation usually takes place in a humid shelter (e.g. a burrow or in the soil) and, like overwintering, involves a significant slowing down of the metabolism.

Allopatry The complete geographic isolation of populations, which can lead to their evolution as different species (i.e. allopatric species).

Amplexus The mating position adopted by many amphibians for breeding. In anurans, amplexus is dorsal: the male grasps the female on the back, either at the armpits (axillary amplexus) or at the waist (lumbar amplexus). In salamanders, amplexus is ventral: the female climbs on the back of the male.

Anuran A member of Anura, the taxonomic order grouping frogs and toads.

Aposematism The strategy of exhibiting vivid colours to advertise toxicity (e.g. as in the Common Fire Salamander). After a bad experience of attempting to ingest a toxic species, predators learn to associate these visual cues with toxicity and therefore avoid preying on the corresponding species.

Bufotoxin The collective name for the group of neurotoxic alkaloids produced by the skin and parotoid glands of true toads, notably in the genus *Bufo*. Bufotoxins serve as defensive chemicals.

Chemoreception The mechanism enabling chemical communication between individuals, notably via pheromones. It is particularly important in newts and salamanders.

Chytridiomycosis An emerging amphibian disease caused by fungal infection of the skin. Symptoms include thickening and reddening of the skin's keratin, preventing breathing and feeding, and affecting endocrinology, ultimately leading to death. It has spread across the globe and no control is available as yet. Some species appear resistant.

Cirri (sing. cirrus) The pair of thin glandular lines running from the nostril to the chin in cave salamanders (*Speleomantes*). The feature plays a central role in chemoreception during courtship.

Cloaca The posterior orifice of amphibians connected to the digestive, reproductive and urinary tracts. In Caudata, its size and shape can vary between sexes and species. Its position can also be used to identify some anuran tadpoles.

Costal groove The depressions formed by the ribs, visible on the external flanks of some salamanders and larvae.

Cryptic species Species that look similar morphologically and cannot readily be identified without genetic tools. However, since these species often evolved through allopatry or parapatry, their distribution ranges do not usually overlap.

Dextral On the right side.

Dorsal On the upper side or back.

Ectotherm An animal that does not produce its own body heat and instead requires external heat sources to regulate its temperature. Amphibians are ectotherms.

Endemism The uniqueness of a species in a particular geographic region.

Explosive breeding A colloquial expression used to characterise amphibians that breed suddenly, in massive numbers, but over a short period of time.

Froglet A small frog that has recently metamorphosed.

Gamete The germ cells transferred for reproduction, i.e. the spermatozoids and eggs. They each contain half the usual number of chromosomes of the species.

Genome The genetic information of individuals, made of chains of DNA (deoxyribonucleic acid) arranged into chromosomes.

Gravid Referring to females carrying unborn progenies (eggs or young), i.e. pregnant.

Gular Referring to the throat.

Hybridogenesis A special reproductive system characteristic of some hybrids, where only half of the genome is transmitted to the next generation, the other half being discarded. In amphibians, it is seen in *Pelophylax*, for example Edible Frogs (page 113), which are hybrids between Pool Frogs (page 105) and Marsh Frogs, and pass on only one parental genome.

Inguinal loop The comma-shaped ending of the lateral line in some tree frog species.

Keratin Fibrous structural proteins found in many tissues. In amphibians, keratin forms hard filaments that strengthen and protect their epidermal skin.

Klepton (abbrev. kl.) A species that relies on another species to complete its reproductive cycle. In European amphibians, hybridogenetic hybrids such as the Edible Frog are kleptons, since they need other water frogs to reproduce.

Labial Tooth Row Formula (LTRF) The number of upper-tooth rows or lower-tooth rows in the mouth of anuran tadpoles.

Larviparity A reproductive strategy whereby the eggs develop and hatch within the mother, which then gives birth directly to larvae (e.g. as in the Common Fire Salamander).

Lateral line The black-and-white stripe running along the flank of some tree frog species, eventually ending in an inguinal loop.

Leg test An ad hoc field assessment of the relative leg size to body size of frogs. It involves projecting the hindlimb above the head and folding the tibia to see how high it reaches (see page 39 for example). It is a particularly useful diagnostic tool for distinguishing between sympatric species of brown frogs.

Lek A group of individuals gathering together to breed. Most anurans breed in leks, with males calling together in chorus to attract females.

Maculation The presence of colour spots.

Maquis A dry shrubland habitat, characteristic of Mediterranean regions.

Metacarpal tubercle The rounded protuberances on the 'hand'. In *Alytes*, the metacarpal tubercles are important for species identification.

Metamorph See 'Metamorphosis'.

Metamorphosis The process during which a larvae transforms into the adult form. It involves major anatomical changes, such as growing limbs, developing lungs and rearranging the entire digestive system. Young frogs that have just completed metamorphosis, but have not yet fully resorbed obsolete larval features such as the tail, are often called metamorphs.

Metatarsal tubercle The rounded protuberance at the base of the 'foot'. Metatarsal tubercles have evolved into different shapes in different species.

Morphotype A special form of some individuals of a species (e.g. of a particular colour or morphology), resulting from environmental, developmental or genetic variation. Several morphotypes may coexist within the same population. Distinct morphotypes found in geographically isolated areas are sometimes considered subspecies.

Neoteny The retention of larval traits such as gills at adulthood, as observed in some newts. It is usually driven by environmental conditions. Maturation may still arise later in life. The Olm is a purely neotenic species, with all individuals retaining gills throughout their life. Also called paedomorphy.

Nuptial pads or calluses Thick protuberances present on the fingers and/or forearms of breeding males in many anuran species. They are usually dark in colour (grey, brown or black) and are resorbed after the reproductive period. Some species also bear them on the throat.

Paedomorphy See 'Neoteny'.

Palearctic The biogeographic realm encompassing Eurasia, North Africa and the Middle East; one of the eight ecozones found on Earth. It is usually divided into the Eastern Palearctic (central and north-east Asia) and the Western Palearctic (the region covered by this book, and including Europe, North Africa and the Middle East).

Parapatry The adjacent ranges of different species, which do not overlap but are in contact at margins. It is the intermediate case between allopatry (isolated ranges) and sympatry (overlapping ranges).

Parotoid glands A pair of cutaneous glands located behind the eyes of anurans and salamanders, which secret bufotoxins. Their size and shape differ between species. Sometimes spelt parotid.

Ploidy The number of chromosome sets of a species. It is usually two (diploid): one inherited from the mother and one inherited from the father. Some amphibians are triploid (three chromosome sets) or tetraploid (four chromosome sets), and gametes are produced in a different manner.

Polytypic A species for which several lineages and/or subspecies have been described.

***Sensu lato* (abbrev. *s.l.*)** Literally meaning 'broad sense', this expression is used to designate a group of cryptic species by the name of the nominal species. For instance, *Hyla arborea s.l.* refers to *H. arborea* and its close relatives *H. molleri, H. orientalis, H. intermedia* and *H. perrini*.

***Sensu stricto* (abbrev. *s.s.*)** Literally meaning 'strict sense', this expression is used to designate only the nominal species of a group of cryptic species. For instance, *Hyla arborea s.s.* refers only to *H. arborea*.

Sinistral On the left side.

Spermatophore In caudata, a capsule of sperm, often shaped like a bag, which is transferred externally or internally to the female during mating.

Spiracle The external respiratory orifice of a tadpole. It can be located on the belly (ventral) or on the left flank (sinistral), and its position and shape vary between species.

Sub-gular Referring to the lower part of the throat.

Sympatry The overlapping ranges of species. Sympatric species are not necessarily syntopic, i.e. if they live in different habitats.

Syntopy The sharing of habitats by different species. Syntopic species are, by extension, sympatric.

Temporal marks Colour patterns located on the forehead (temple) in ranid frogs.

Thermoregulation The ability to adjust body temperature. In ectothermic species like amphibians, it is achieved by specific behaviours (e.g. exposure to the sun) and by physiological changes (e.g. skin darkening to absorb more solar energy).

Toadlet A small toad that has recently metamorphosed.

Triploid See 'Ploidy'.

Tubercle A small bony or keratinised protuberance found on the skin surface, notably on the palms.

Tympanum The eardrum, seen in anurans as a lateral disc next to the eye.

Unken reflex The defensive posture adopted in the face of danger by some amphibians (e.g. *Bombina*) to advertise their colourful underparts and signal their toxicity.

Urodele A member of the order Caudata (or Urodela), the taxonomic order grouping salamanders and newts.

Ventral On the underside.

Viviparity A reproductive strategy whereby the eggs and larvae develop internally in the mother, which gives birth to fully formed young (e.g. as in the Alpine Salamander,). Note that, technically, amphibians are ovoviviparous, because embryos are not nourished by the mother via a placenta, instead relying on yolk.

Western Palearctic See 'Palearctic'.

Xeric A very dry environment, like the Mediterranean maquis.

ANURA

Alytidae

The family Alytidae (formerly Discoglossidae) includes two distinct groups of Mediterranean species from south-western Europe: the midwife toads from the genus *Alytes* (five species) and the painted frogs from the genus *Discoglossus* (six species). An additional species from Israel – the Hula Painted Frog – belongs to an otherwise extinct genus, *Latonia* (see page 41).

Midwife toads could be considered feminists; their names owing to their famous male parental care behaviour. Males wrap the eggs around their hindlimbs, and keep their progeny safe by carrying the clutch, releasing them only once they are ready to hatch – usually in shallow, narrow, yet permanent water puddles. As such, they are essentially terrestrial, often hidden in sandy burrows but revealing their presence by whistling mating calls. Midwife toads are poisonous due to the small warts covering their skin, and hence have few predators.

With their smooth skin, pointy head and more aquatic habits, *Discoglossus* more closely resemble frogs. As their name implies, painted frogs have colourful markings that are reminiscent of military uniforms. They occupy a variety of habitats, including temperate forests, Mediterranean scrublands, rivers, swamps and marshes. Painted toads breed almost all year long, relying on various water bodies often associated with traditional agriculture, for example, irrigation ditches and cattle tracks. As a result, the modernisation of agricultural practices poses a major threat to their survival.

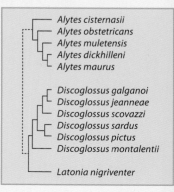

Alytes cisternasii
Alytes obstetricans
Alytes muletensis
Alytes dickhilleni
Alytes maurus

Discoglossus galganoi
Discoglossus jeanneae
Discoglossus scovazzi
Discoglossus sardus
Discoglossus pictus
Discoglossus montalentii

Latonia nigriventer

Left This male midwife toad just received a fresh batch of eggs from the last female he mated with; he is about to bury himself in the ground to ensure that they develop safely.

Right The Tyrrhenian Painted Frog inhabits the Western Mediterranean basin and comes in three different morphs: striped, spotted (as seen here) and uniform.

Left The very rare Hula Painted Frog was thought to be extinct for the past 70 years, before a park ranger rediscovered it during a routine patrol in 2014.

Left During mating, the male Common Midwife Toad grasps the eggs on its back.

Right The tadpoles can grow enormous as they often overwinter.

Common Midwife Toad – *Alytes obstetricans*

The Common Midwife Toad has colonised dry Mediterranean scrublands, finding a home in tiny water bodies such as fountains, reservoirs and the remaining puddles of dry streams, where its tadpoles are seen quivering in the shallows. These develop slowly and often overwinter, when different age classes may coexist – some reach enormous sizes, when they may be confused with large *Pelophylax* or *Pelobates* tadpoles. Four subspecies are distributed across Spain, although their exact status and distribution are pending further analyses.

Identification Criteria
1. Small, stocky toad-like shape with tiny parotoid glands
2. Large eyes with a vertical slit-shaped pupil
3. Orange warts

Size: 3–5cm
Habitat: Usually found in dry, sunny environments, including cultivated areas, gravel pits, rocky slopes and forests with tiny water bodies; up to 2,400m in the Pyrenees
Reproductive Period: May–August
Sexual Dimorphism: There are no clear morphological differences, but males carry the eggs
Call: From a terrestrial hiding place, emits a high-pitched, explosive, musical, whistling *pee… pee… pee…* with intervals of a few seconds; can be confused with the call of a Scops Owl (*Otus scops*) or Pygmy Owl (*Glaucidium passerinum*)
Spawn: Eggs yellowish, carried by males; clutches usually of 30–60 eggs
Tadpoles: Already large at hatching (>1cm) and can grow to 9cm; spiracle mid-ventral; nostrils closer to snout tip than eyes; greyish with random pigmentation on the tail muscle; LTRF 2/3
Subspecies: Four (page 192)
IUCN Red List: Least Concern

Left Embryos develop on the back of the male.

Right Unlike other *Alytes*, *Alytes cisternasii* has only two tubercles on the palm.

Iberian Midwife Toad – *Alytes cisternasii*

The Iberian Midwife Toad is endemic to south-western parts of the Iberian Peninsula, where it inhabits xeric environments with sandy-granitic soils such as light oak forests, yet still remaining close to temporary streams. The species reproduces in the autumn and its tadpoles take only a few months to metamorphose. Males control the humidity of the eggs by adapting the depth and diameter of their burrow. Sympatric with *Alytes obstetricans boscai* in northern regions, the Iberian Midwife Toad can easily be distinguished by its reddish darts and by having two tubercles in its palm (three in other *Alytes*). It is threatened by habitat destruction and chytridiomycosis.

Identification Criteria
Similar to Common Midwife Toad (page 30) but:
① Two metacarpal tubercles
② Reddish warts
③ White line between the eyes often present

Size: 3–5cm
Habitat: Dry lowland areas with little precipitation, including sunny slopes and cultivated areas; usually close to houses and water sources; up to 1,500m
Reproductive Period: September–March (peak in October–November)
Sexual Dimorphism: As for Common Midwife Toad
Call: Similar to Common Midwife Toad, but calls heard in late autumn and winter are likely to be this species
Spawn: As for Common Midwife Toad
Tadpoles: Similar to Common Midwife Toad, but dark patches on the tail muscle form one or two lines
IUCN Red List: Near Threatened

Left This species, the only midwife toad in south-eastern Spain, lacks colourful warts.

Betic Midwife Toad – *Alytes dickhilleni*

Sometimes also called the Southern Midwife Toad, this species is restricted to isolated patches of pine–oak woodlands in the Betic Mountains of south-eastern Spain. Described as recently as 1995, it differs from other midwife toads in its uniform grey coloration and lack of coloured warts. The larval stage usually lasts for more than a year and therefore requires a high-quality permanent water body; the Betic Midwife Toad is thus particularly threatened by climate change in this dry part of Europe. Eighty per cent of the remaining populations breed in water tanks or cattle troughs in disconnected valleys, and the species is also highly sensitive to chytridiomycosis.

Identification Criteria
Similar to Common Midwife Toad (page 30) but:
① Dusty appearance with uniform grey coloration
② Warts are grey or black, not coloured

Size: 3–5cm
Habitat: Mountainous areas, usually with pine–oak forests on steep terrain; altitudes of 500–2,300m
Reproductive Period: Almost year-round, from December–August
Sexual Dimorphism: As for Common Midwife Toad
Call: As for Common Midwife Toad
Spawn: As for Common Midwife Toad
Tadpoles: Similar to Common Midwife Toad, but dark patches form a line on the top of the tail muscles, reaching to the body
IUCN Red List: Vulnerable

Left This tiny species is more slender than other *Alytes*, with a pointy snout.

Right Tadpoles can take three years to reach metamorphosis.

Majorcan Midwife Toad – *Alytes muletensis*

The Majorcan Midwife Toad is one of the most highly protected amphibians in Europe, with about 500 breeding pairs known from only 10 streams in the Serra de Tramuntana mountain range in Majorca. It was first described from fossil records, before the live animals were discovered in 1979. The species inhabits streams in limestone caverns and is particularly adapted to its extremely dry environment. It has a smaller, more flattened body than other *Alytes*, and hides underneath boulders and in narrow crevices. Threatened by introduced predators (snakes and large frogs), the species has been maintained through the reintroduction of captive-bred individuals since the 1980s.

Identification Criteria
1. Less stocky and with longer legs than other midwife toads
2. Smooth skin
3. Greyish yellow with marbled blackish-green spots

Size: 3–4cm
Habitat: Narrow canyons in limestone massifs with streams that form puddles in the summer; hides in crevices or under rocks
Reproductive Period: April–June
Sexual Dimorphism: As for Common Midwife Toad (page 30)
Call: Melodic *pi… pi… pi…*, like drops of water falling in a bucket; usually nocturnal but can also be heard calling during the day
Spawn: Eggs are larger than in other *Alytes*, but clutches are smaller, usually <20 eggs
Tadpoles: Similar to Common Midwife Toad, but nostrils are closer to the eyes than to the snout tip, and upper tail fin is lower than the body height; can stay in the larval stage up to three years
IUCN Red List: Vulnerable

Left Moroccan midwife toads aestivate by burrowing themselves in the ground.

Moroccan Midwife Toad – *Alytes maurus*

This Moroccan endemic is morphologically similar to the Common Midwife Toad (page 30) and was long considered the same species. Its tadpoles differ in their pigment networks and buccal features, but genetic and osteological data were instrumental in raising its taxonomic status to species level. Only about 20 fragmented localities are known, from the central Atlas and central Rif mountains in north-eastern Morocco. The species is locally threatened by water pollution and introduced fish (especially the Eastern Mosquitofish, *Gambusia holbrooki*), which prey on the tadpoles, as well as habitat fragmentation and climate change.

Identification Criteria
Morphologically identical to Common Midwife Toad and distinguishable only by distribution (see map)

Size: 3–5cm
Habitat: Humid areas in karst, boulders and escarpments with maquis vegetation, and open forests, close to permanent streams or pools; altitudes of 200–2,100m
Reproductive Period: Not clear; calls heard February–April
Sexual Dimorphism: As for Common Midwife Toad
Call: Similar to Common Midwife Toad, although significantly shorter
Spawn: As for Common Midwife Toad
Tadpoles: Similar to Common Midwife Toad, but with a conspicuous pattern of dark and golden spots
IUCN Red List: Near Threatened

Left Uniform morph of *Discoglossus pictus*.

Right Spotted morph of *Discoglossus pictus*.

Painted Frog – *Discoglossus pictus*

The Painted Frog can be found in a wide array of Mediterranean habitats, especially human-associated landscapes, where it uses irrigation channels, ponds or water cisterns in vineyards, pastures and cultivated fields for breeding. Three morphs coexist: uniformly coloured, striped and spotted. The species breeds almost year-round, especially in the Maghreb, and females can lay up to six full clutches in a year. They are highly promiscuous and can copulate with several males in one night, each time spawning a small grape-like cluster of 20–50 eggs. The presence of the African subspecies *Discoglossus pictus auritus* in Catalonia is a result of introductions in the nineteenth century.

Identification Criteria
1. Vertical teardrop-shaped pupil
2. Tympanum discreet but visible
3. Grey, brown or green coloration
4. Longitudinal stripes or dark spots with bright edges

Size: 4–8cm
Habitat: All types of Mediterranean habitats, usually close to shallow water bodies; mostly in lowlands, but up to 1,500m in Sicily
Reproductive Period: Almost year-round, from October to July
Sexual Dimorphism: Males are slightly larger than females and have smoother skin; breeding males have dark calluses on the first fingers, throat and belly
Call: Series of fast, shy, grumpy-sounding *rar… rar… rar* notes emitted from the water's surface or even underwater, usually at night
Spawn: Eggs dark brown, 6–8mm in diameter; laid in grape-like clusters of 20–50 on the floor of the water body or on aquatic vegetation
Tadpoles: Dark; <c.3.5cm; spiracle mid-ventral; tail tip round; fine network of dark polygonal meshes on the fin; LTRF 2/3
Subspecies: Two (page 193)
IUCN Red List: Least Concern

Left Colourful striped morphs are commonly found in this species.

Moroccan Painted Frog – *Discoglossus scovazzi*

This species diverged from other *Discoglossus* about five million years ago following the opening of the Strait of Gibraltar and subsequent filling of the Mediterranean Sea. A precocious species, the Moroccan Painted Frog starts breeding with the first winter rains (October). It is common throughout its range, especially in humid or sub-humid areas, but can be threatened by habitat destruction through land conversion. It is unclear whether the species overlaps and hybridises with the Painted Frog (page 35) in eastern Morocco, but their ranges have probably remained separate throughout the Quaternary due to episodes of drought.

Identification Criteria
Morphologically identical to Painted Frog and distinguishable only by distribution (see map)

Size: 4–8cm
Habitat: Small water bodies such as temporary ponds, springs, ditches, vehicle tracks and slow-flowing streams
Reproductive Period: October–January in the lowlands, as late as June in the highlands; up to 2,600m
Sexual Dimorphism: As for Painted Frog
Call: Similar to Painted Frog, but shorter and the series usually lacks intervals
Spawn/Tadpoles: Supposedly similar to Painted Frog, but systematic description is lacking
IUCN Red List: Least Concern

Right Like other painted frogs, *Discoglossus galganoi* can be found with spotted or, like this individual, striped colour patterns.

Iberian Painted Frog – *Discoglossus galganoi*

The Iberian Painted Frog is a ubiquitous, abundant species throughout its range across Portugal and western Spain. It occurs in a variety of humid habitats, usually in the direct vicinity of water bodies such as swamps, streams, and even stagnant and brackish pools. It features some genetic, biochemical and subtle morphometric differences from its east Iberian counterpart, the Spanish Painted Frog (page 38), but reliable identification in the field is virtually impossible and geographic location remains the sole decisive criterion. The transition between the two species occurs in central Iberia, delimited by the Guadalquivir River in the south and saline lakes in the centre.

Identification Criteria
Similar to Painted Frog (page 35) but:
① Tympanum almost invisible

Size: 4–8cm
Habitat: Various aquatic habitats in granitic massifs, such as ponds, swamps and wetlands; streams in mountainous areas; up to 1,800m
Reproductive Period: Almost year-round, from October to July
Sexual Dimorphism: As for Painted Frog
Call: Similar to Painted Frog but individual croaks are longer
Spawn/Tadpoles: As for Painted Frog
IUCN Red List: Least Concern

Left *Discoglossus jeanneae* features similar coloration and morphology to *D. galganoi.*

Right Like other *Discoglossus*, males display dark calluses on the fingers.

Spanish Painted Frog – *Discoglossus jeanneae*

Described in 1986 following detailed comparative analyses with the Iberian Painted Frog (page 37), this species is the eastern Iberian equivalent of the former and shares a similar biology. No field criteria other than geography are reliable for distinguishing the two. The potential history of hybridisation between *Discoglossus jeanneae* is often considered a subspecies of *D. galganoi* with which it seems to hybridise in Central Spain. The distribution of the Spanish Painted Frog is patchy, and many populations live in arid environments; the species is impacted by the increasing occurrence of droughts. Yet, it is more common in the southern parts of its range and scarce in the north.

Identification Criteria
Morphologically identical to Iberian Painted Frog and distinguishable only by distribution (see map)

Size: 4–7cm
Habitat: Limestone and gypsum massifs with pine groves and shrubland, and with various types of water bodies; up to 2,000m
Reproductive Period: Almost year round, from October–July
Sexual Dimorphism: As for Painted Frog (page 35)
Call: Similar to Painted Frog but individual croaks are longer
Spawn/Tadpoles: As for Painted Frog
IUCN Red List: Near Threatened

Left This species usually has dark coloration or, at the very least, dark blotches.

Right *Discoglossus montalentii* is particularly present in upland streams.

Corsican Painted Frog – *Discoglossus montalentii*

Unlike most other *Discoglossus* species, the Corsican Painted Frog comes in only two colour morphs: uniform or spotted (without bright edges). Endemic to Corsica, it is found in fast-flowing upland streams and water bodies in forests in the central mountain ranges. It shares the island with the Tyrrhenian Painted Frog (page 40), but the presence of this species in Corsica was not known until recently and previous studies on the Corsican Painted Frog may very well have included the former. The two species can be syntopic, but the Corsican Painted Frog is more usually found in the highlands. Their colour markings are also similar, but they can be distinguished by their snout profile and fingertips.

Identification Criteria
1. Dark brown/grey or reddish colour
2. Spotted morphs have dark spots with dull edges
3. Rounded, spatula-shaped fingertips, usually forming a ball on the fourth finger
4. Rounded snout profile, with upper and lower edges parallel
5. Long hindlimbs (leg test: reaching up between the eyes and the snout extremity)

Size: 4–6.5cm
Habitat: Fast-flowing streams in forest areas; altitudes of 300–1,900m
Reproductive Period: Presumably April–July
Sexual Dimorphism: As for Painted Frog (page 35)
Call: *Poop… poop… poop*, reminiscent of that of Yellow-bellied Toad (page 44); more musical than other *Discoglossus*
Spawn/Tadpoles: Supposedly similar to Painted Frog
IUCN Red List: Near Threatened

Left Tadpoles of this species are dark with fine lines on the tail.

Right This species chooses water bodies with good exposure to the sun.

Tyrrhenian Painted Frog – *Discoglossus sardus*

As its vernacular name implies, this species is distributed on several islands in the Tyrrhenian Sea, including Corsica (where it coexists with the Corsican Painted Frog; page 39), the Maddalena archipelago, San Pietro, Hyères, Giglio and Montecristo. Populations are also established on the Monte Argentario Peninsula in mainland Tuscany, likely following human introductions. Although the species is abundant overall, small insular populations may decline rapidly following human disturbance due to their poor genetic diversity and isolated nature. The species is sometimes found together with the Italian Pool Frog (page 101), but is easily distinguished by its coloration and pupil shape.

Identification Criteria

Similar to Corsican Painted Frog but:

1. Fourth finger on each forefoot is tapering, not spatula-shaped
2. Snout profile pointy, leaning on the lower edge
3. Hindlimbs shorter (leg test: reaching only up to the eyes)

Size: 4–7cm
Habitat: Sunny water bodies, including wetlands, ponds and calm streams; sometimes in maquis and forests; up to 1,300m (Corsica) and 1,770m (Sardinia)
Reproductive Period: March–August
Sexual Dimorphism: As for Painted Frog (page 35)
Call: As for Painted Frog
Spawn/Tadpoles: As for Painted Frog
IUCN Red List: Least Concern

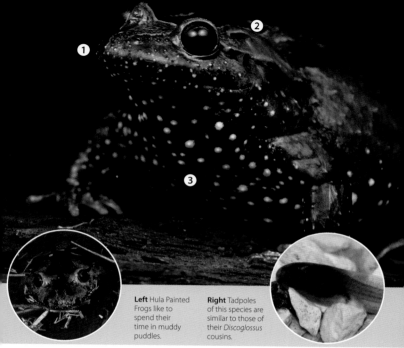

Left Hula Painted Frogs like to spend their time in muddy puddles.

Right Tadpoles of this species are similar to those of their *Discoglossus* cousins.

Hula Painted Frog – *Latonia nigriventer*

First described in 1943, the Hula Painted Frog disappeared soon after in the 1950s and was the first amphibian to be declared Extinct in the Wild by the IUCN. However, it made headlines in life sciences magazines in 2011 when it was rediscovered, and again in 2013 when analyses revealed that it was the only surviving member of the genus *Latonia*, otherwise known only from fossil records. The species, endemic to Lake Hula in Israel (in an area of less than 3km²), likely suffered from the drainage of the lake in the 1950s and then subsequently recovered thanks to long-term rehydration of the marshes and protection of the area as a nature reserve.

Identification Criteria
① Robust frog with dull coloration
② Flat head with heart-shaped iris
③ Black/grey belly with white spots

Size: 7–13cm
Habitat: Shallow waterholes or ditches along the swampy shores of Lake Hula
Reproductive Period: Prolonged, potentially February–September
Sexual Dimorphism: Body size is similar in males and female; during the breeding period, males display dark nuptial pads as well as hundreds of tiny black excrescences on the thorax, arms, thighs and plantar surfaces
Call: Similar to Painted Frog (page 35), but low in pitch and at a very low intensity
Spawn: Never witnessed, but probably similar to Painted Frog
Tadpoles: Brown with unpigmented ventral side; spiracle mid-ventral; dense network of black lines on tail; LTRF 2/3
IUCN Red List: Critically Endangered

Above When mating, the male clasps the female at the waist.

Above and right *Bombina* toads lay tiny clumps of eggs attached to the vegetation. The tadpoles hatch in less than two months.

Bombinatoridae

The Latin word *bombinator*, the root of the family name Bombinatoridae, can be translated as 'buzzer', a reference to the gentle musical note these amphibians emit in chorus while breeding. In English, they are commonly known as fire-bellied toads due to their coloured ventral sides. Two genera are known: *Barbourula*, the jungle toads, with two known species endemic to the Philippines and Borneo; and *Bombina*, members of which are widespread in Eurasia. Among the six *Bombina* species recognised, three occur in Europe: Fire-bellied Toad (*Bombina bombina*), Yellow-bellied Toad (*B. variegata*) and Apennine Yellow-bellied Toad (*B. pachypus*). The ecology of members of the two genera varies greatly, with *Barbourula* being restricted to jungle forests and *Bombina* inhabiting either steppes and open wetlands (Fire-bellied Toad), or more wooded areas (Yellow-bellied Toad).

Bombinatorids are small (<6cm) aquatic amphibians, with triangular or heart-shaped pupils. Their dull greyish skin is covered with warts, and provides a particularly good camouflage. In contrast, their colourful bellies signal their high toxicity. When disturbed, and especially in the face of an imminent predator attack, *Bombina* toads arch their body and limbs upward to display their ventral colours. This behaviour, known as the unken reflex, warns predators about their poisonous nature in order to discourage attack. In the course of the reflex, the toad also releases antibacterial and antifungal toxins, and swallows air to bloat itself in an attempt to look larger. During the breeding season, males gather in choruses of up to thousands of individuals. Females lay 50–300 eggs on aquatic vegetation, usually in small clumps of a few at a time. *Bombina* species are widespread in central and eastern Europe, but are regionally threatened in western Europe due to habitat loss.

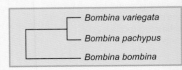

Bombina variegata
Bombina pachypus
Bombina bombina

Left Belly colour patterns are used to warn predators about the toxicity of the toad.

Right In order to attract females, males call but also inflate their body to appear larger.

Fire-bellied Toad – *Bombina bombina*

The largest member of the Bombinatoridae family, the Fire-bellied Toad inhabits the open forests, plains, wetlands and steppes of central and eastern Europe. It has a mainly aquatic lifestyle, favouring shallow water bodies such as flooded fields, where it is active day and night. As in other *Bombina* species, the ventral colour pattern of each individual is unique and can be used for identification in capture–recapture studies. The echoing calls of Fire-bellied Toad choruses have even inspired some music composers. The species is locally threatened by pollution and destruction of its wetlands habitats, particularly in western parts of its range.

Identification Criteria
① Flattened grey body
② Heart-shaped pupil
③ Black belly with orange/red patches, sometimes mottled
④ Groin and thigh colour patches unconnected

Size: 3–5cm
Habitat: Open lowland wetlands, swamps and shallow edges of ponds with subaquatic vegetation; up to 750m
Reproductive Period: April–August
Sexual Dimorphism: Breeding males have several brownish nuptial calluses on the inner side of the forearms and first fingers
Call: Intense, explosive *oohh… oohh… oohh…* with intervals of 2–4 seconds, like a hunting horn; large choruses heard from a distance are reminiscent of a pealing bell; males call from the water during the afternoon and evening
Spawn: Egg diameter 5–8mm; deposited in small spawns of <30 eggs on aquatic vegetation
Tadpoles: <5cm; spiracle ventral on rear of body; high and long upper tail fin, reaching the eyes; fin tip rounded; mouth triangular; LTRF 2/3
IUCN Red List: Least Concern

Left *Bombina variegata* has much more yellow on the belly than *B. bombina*.

Right The unken reflex consists of the toad stretching its limbs and back to display is bright underparts.

Yellow-bellied Toad – *Bombina variegata*

While the ventral side of the Fire-bellied Toad (page 43) is dark with coloured spots, in the Yellow-bellied Toad it is coloured with dark spots. The two also differ in their social behaviour – the Yellow-bellied gathers in large groups, whereas the Fire-bellied is territorial; and by ecology – the Yellow-bellied is more terrestrial and inhabits woodland areas, reaching high elevations in coniferous mountain forests. The Yellow-bellied also lives happily in temporary shallow puddles, like those created in the tracks left by forestry trucks. Southern populations belong to a different subspecies (*Bombina variegata scabra*), characterised by dark dots.

Identification Criteria
Similar to Fire-bellied Toad but:
1. Yellow belly with dark patches
2. Groin and thigh colour patches connected

Size: 3–5cm
Habitat: Flooded areas, wetlands and woodlands, and sometimes human-altered habitats, usually with a mosaic of small, shallow water bodies; up to 2,100m
Reproductive Period: April–August
Sexual Dimorphism: As for Fire-bellied Toad
Call: Similar to Fire-bellied Toad but less intense and faster (intervals of 1–2 seconds); calls are made during both day and night
Spawn: As for Fire-bellied Toad
Tadpoles: Similar to Fire-bellied Toad but with a heart-shaped mouth and shorter tail; upper tail fin is much shorter
Subspecies: Two (page 194)
IUCN Red List: Least Concern

Right This species can also be found in the puddles of fresh mountain streams.

Apennine Yellow-bellied Toad – *Bombina pachypus*

Endemic to Italy, this largely diurnal species can be found in both terrestrial and freshwater habitats, usually in forests but also in open areas such as irrigation ditches in farmlands and on pasture. The breeding season is prolonged, lasting until September, but individuals do not breed continuously throughout the season. Females lay several tiny clutches in different ponds. Unlike the Yellow-bellied Toad (page 44), the Apennine Yellow-bellied appears to be sensitive to chytridiomycosis; it was the first amphibian diagnosed with the infection, in 2001, and infected specimens are symptomatic and face high mortality rates. Other threats include habitat destruction due to changes in agricultural practices.

Identification Criteria
Similar to Yellow-bellied Toad but:
① Ventral sides appear darker

Size: 3–5cm
Habitat: Unshaded ponds and ditches in forests and open areas; up to 1,700m
Reproductive Period: May–September
Sexual Dimorphism: As for Fire-bellied Toad (page 43)
Call: As for Yellow-bellied Toad
Spawn/Tadpoles: As for Yellow-bellied Toad
IUCN Red List: Endangered

Above and left
Parsley frogs have various greenish camouflage. The amplexus is lumbar.

Pelodytidae

A small family of small frogs, Pelodytidae is represented by a single genus, *Pelodytes*, commonly known as the parsley frogs owing to their green-spotted colouring. It is an ancient group, diverging from Pelobatidae about 150 million years ago, when the Earth was dominated by dinosaurs. It was limited to two species for a long time, but recent genetic studies have nearly tripled the *Pelodytes* diversity with new cryptic taxa endemic to Iberia.

Parsley frogs differ from *Pelobates* species in a number of features, including their small size and reduced foot webbing. They also breed by lumbar amplexus, but their sexual dimorphism differs, with males forming dark calluses on their forearms and first fingers (more like bombinatorids), as well as on their chest. Clutches are spawned in gelatinous bands, and smell like fish.

Most of the diversity is in Iberia and nearby France, which are home to four species with disruptive distributions: Common Parsley Frog (*Pelodytes punctatus*), Iberian Parsley Frog (*P. ibericus*), Lusitanian Parsley Frog (*P. hespericus*) and

Above These tiny species are easily heard but very hard to locate, and are often hidden in the mud or grass, as seen here with this Common Parsley Frog.

Hesperides' Parsley Frog (*P. atlanticus*). One deeply diverged species is isolated around the eastern shores of the Caspian Sea: Caucasian Parsley Frog (*P. caucasicus*).

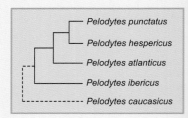

Pelodytes punctatus
Pelodytes hespericus
Pelodytes atlanticus
Pelodytes ibericus
Pelodytes caucasicus

Left *Pelodytes* tadpoles are often seen in very shallow puddles with vegetation.

Right Dark calluses appear on the arms and fingers of breeding males.

Common Parsley Frog – *Pelodytes punctatus*

Common but threatened, the Common Parsley Frog forms fragmented populations in northern Spain, France and north-eastern Italy, usually in open cultivated areas or dry forests. Individuals are tiny and hard to spot, with only their squeaking croaks revealing their presence. Once found, their slender shape, colourful skin and fine profile make them amazing subjects for macro photography. In southern ranges, some individuals breed in autumn rather than spring, but some also breed in both seasons. Common Parsley Frogs are good swimmers and also good climbers, being able to scale smooth vertical surfaces. They also often smell like garlic.

Identification Criteria
1. Vertical pupil
2. Greyish coloration tinted with parsley-coloured patches
3. Longitudinally aligned warts, these are sometimes orange
4. Little or no foot webbing
5. Long hindlimbs (leg test: reaching between the eyes and snout)
6. Flattened palm tubercle

Size: 3–4cm
Habitat: Open cultivated meadows, and pine or oak forests; breeds in shallow waters with vegetation, including tiny streams, flooded fields and puddles
Reproductive Period: February–April and September–October
Sexual Dimorphism: Females are generally larger than males; males have brown nuptial calluses on the forearms and first fingers
Call: Males emit a vibrating, squeaking, scraping *cre-e-e-e-k* above water, reminiscent of a table-tennis ball bouncing between the bat and table; sometimes also a *co-ak… co-ak* underwater; essentially nocturnal
Spawn: Small, messy strings, 20–50cm long, stretched on the vegetation (up to 400 eggs per clutch)
Tadpoles: Light coloured; <7cm (rarely to 10cm); spiracle sinistral; white beak with black lips; LTRF 4/5; cloaca median; tail tip rounded
IUCN Red List: —

Left *Pelodytes* clutches look like elongated grapes, stretched in the vegetation.

Right Parsley frogs appear grey with parsley-coloured patches.

Iberian Parsley Frog – *Pelodytes ibericus*

This species is local to southern Iberia, specifically Andalusia and parts of Extremadura in Spain, and central and southern Portugal. Since it was described recently (2000), the status of many peripheral populations is yet to be determined – especially since it seems to hybridise locally with its neighbours, the Lusitanian Parsley Frog (page 49) in Portugal and Hesperides' Parsley Frog (page 50) in south-western Spain. The species is tolerant of a degree of salinity, sometimes breeding in salty coastal wetlands. The tadpoles are predators of the embryos of other anurans.

Identification Criteria

Similar to Common Parsley Frog (page 47) but:
1. Hindlimbs generally smaller and shorter (leg test: reaching to the eyes)
2. Conical palm tubercle

Size: 3–4cm
Habitat: Similar to Common Parsley Frog but usually found in more ephemeral water bodies; up to 600m
Reproductive Period: October–March
Sexual Dimorphism: As for Common Parsley Frog
Call: Similar to Common Parsley Frog, although sequence length varies; does not usually call underwater
Spawn/Tadpoles: As for Common Parsley Frog
IUCN Red List: Least Concern

Left The typical habitat of this species is wet meadows, as seen here.

Right The colour patterns of the back are highly variable.

Lusitanian Parsley Frog – *Pelodytes atlanticus*

A newly described species restricted to the Atlantic coast of Portugal, the Lusitanian Parsley Frog cannot be separated from the neighbouring Iberian Parsley Frog (page 48) on morphological or acoustic criteria. Because these two species can be distinguished only using genetic tools, the exact boundaries between their distributions are not fully known and deserve further studies. The elevation of the Lusitanian Parsley Frog to species level is too recent for an accurate understanding of its conservation status; however, it is likely be under threat, given the loss of breeding sites in Portugal and the expansion of invasive species like the Signal Crayfish (*Pacifastacus leniusculus*).

Identification Criteria
Morphologically identical to Common Parsley Frog (page 47) and distinguishable only by distribution (see map)

Size: 3–4cm
Habitat: Similar to Iberian Parsley Frog; mostly temporary ponds in traditional Mediterranean farmland
Reproductive Period: October–March
Sexual Dimorphism: As for Common Parsley Frog
Call: As for Common Parsley Frog
Spawn/Tadpoles: As for Common Parsley Frog
IUCN Red List: —

Left Finding this tiny frog requires close inspection of the water body shores from where it calls.

Hesperides' Parsley Frog – *Pelodytes hespericus*

The recently described Hesperides' Parsley Frog is widespread throughout south-western Spain, where it is commonly found in abandoned quarries and cattle ponds. Although genetics and/or distribution are the sole definitive criteria for identifying the species, its mating call sounds as if it is suddenly interrupted, in contrast with the longer sequences of its relatives. Isolated for at least three million years, the species has survived arid episodes during the Quaternary and expanded southwards to Andalusia (where it meets with the Iberian Parsley Frog; page 48), as well as northwards to Catalonia (where it meets the Common Parsley Frog; page 47).

Identification Criteria
Morphologically identical to Common Parsley Frog and distinguishable only by distribution (see map)

Size: 3–4cm
Habitat: Permanent or ephemeral shallow water bodies in steppe or light forest areas
Reproductive Period: October–March
Sexual Dimorphism: As for Common Parsley Frog
Call: Similar to Common Parsley Frog but shorter: *cre-ek*
Spawn/Tadpoles: As for Common Parsley Frog
IUCN Red List: —

Right A resident of the humid Caucasian forests, this species is more stockily built than other *Pelodytes*.

Caucasian Parsley Frog – *Pelodytes caucasicus*

Unlike its western Mediterranean relatives, the Caucasian Parsley Frog is a forest species, inhabiting woodlands in the Caucasus and Anatolia, and preferring cool, shaded conditions. Both adults and tadpoles hibernate for several months to survive the harsh winter, and some tadpoles even overwinter for two years consecutively. The breeding period is initiated by the rising temperature of running waters, and can be very long. This species is threatened by the clearing of forests, water contamination by pesticides, and predation by invasive raccoons (*Procyon lotor*).

Identification Criteria
(1) Crenellated skin
(2) More stocky build than in other parsley frogs

Size: 4–5cm
Habitat: Humid habitats in broad-leaved or mixed forests on the banks of shaded streams, creeks and ponds; up to 1,800m
Reproductive Period: May–October
Sexual Dimorphism: As for Common Parsley Frog (page 47)
Call: Similar to Common Parsley Frog but longer and more clicking *cllle-e-e-k*
Spawn/Tadpoles: Generally similar to Common Parsley Frog
IUCN Red List: Near Threatened

Pelobatidae

Following recent taxonomic revisions, the Pelobatidae family now contains a single genus, the Western Palearctic *Pelobates*. These relatively large, chubby amphibians are known as burrowing toads. They live in loose sandy soils and dig holes with their hind feet to burrow themselves in, emerging for feeding and breeding. They are particularly well adapted to this lifestyle: they use their massive, thick skull to burst their way out of the ground, and their hind feet are equipped with a long, sharp, keratinised tubercle, which acts as a spade for digging.

Breeding takes place in spring, usually in temporary shallow ponds with vegetation. Amplexus is lumbar, and clutches consist of strings in which eggs are randomly arranged, not in rows as in the bufonids. Desiccation of the pond is a risk faced by tadpoles, but sometimes they delay metamorphosis and grow to enormous sizes (>10cm).

The species occur in Morocco (Moroccan Spadefoot, *Pelobates varaldii*), Iberia (Western Spadefoot, *P. cultripes*), central and eastern Europe (Common, Pallas's and

Above Spadefoot toads are lowland, steppic species inhabiting large marshes with sandy soil, such as the Nesto Delta in Greece (shown here).

Balkans spadefoots, *P. fuscus*, *P. vespertinus* and *P. balcanicus*) and Asia Minor (Eastern Spadefoot, *P. syriacus*). They are easily distinguished from other anurans by the blades on their hind feet; vertical pupils; smooth skin; and the lack of parotoid glands.

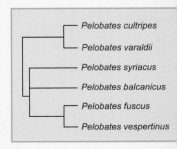

Pelobates cultripes
Pelobates varaldii
Pelobates syriacus
Pelobates balcanicus
Pelobates fuscus
Pelobates vespertinus

Right Spadefoot toads spend a lot of time on the ground. However, they are also aquatic – especially during the breeding season.

Above In *Pelobates*, the amplexus is lumbar, with the male clasping the females around the waist, as seen here with these Common Spadefoot toads.

Right The Iberian Western Spadefoot has very visible black blades on its hind feet.

Left The tubercles of spadefoots have evolved into a blade that is used for digging.

Right Clutches form loose, messy cords containing thousands of eggs.

Western Spadefoot – *Pelobates cultripes*

Essentially nocturnal, the Western Spadefoot unearths itself from its sandy burrow after sunset, when it may be found wandering around in search of small insect prey. Once disturbed, it may try to reburrow itself, a task accomplished in a matter of minutes thanks to its spades. If threatened, it will inflate its body like a balloon and scream with a surprisingly intense, yet amazingly cute, kitten-like mewling sound. Its breeding is explosive, initiated by rain showers. Tadpoles can grow enormous, up to 12cm. Adults may gather to breed several times during the year, but their activity is linked to local rainfall regimes.

Identification Criteria
1. Chubby with smooth skin
2. Bulging eyes with vertical pupils
3. Flat skull
4. Black spade under the hind feet
5. Variable coloration, orange spots usually absent or rare

Size: 6–10cm
Habitat: Open areas with soft or sandy soil, usually in lowlands; near small, shallow, temporary water bodies with vegetation, sometimes in small springs
Reproductive Period: October–April
Sexual Dimorphism: Males have oval protuberances on their arms and pearly granules on their forearms and hands
Call: Monotonous, smooth clinking, *co-co-co*, sometimes emitted underwater; reminiscent of a chicken's cackling; distress call is an intense, piercing, high-pitched, continuous *hiiiieeeeeee*
Spawn: Eggs greyish; arranged randomly in sausage-like strings up to 1m long (up to 7,000 eggs)
Tadpoles: Very large (8–10cm, to >12cm); body globular, golden-bronze coloration; LTRF 4/5; large inter-eye distance; spiracle sinistral and diagonally oriented upward; cloaca median; relatively high upper tail fin; mouth black; tail tip very pointy; tubercle already visible in old tadpoles
IUCN Red List: Near Threatened

Left The bulging eyes of this species can reflect a flashlight from a great distance.

Right The eyelids are speckled with orange dots.

Moroccan Spadefoot – *Pelobates varaldii*

This Moroccan endemic is known only from fragmented populations along the north-western coastal plains of the country. Although the species is abundant in the north, its isolated southern populations – which live in barren environments – are highly threatened. Categorised as Endangered by the IUCN, the Moroccan Spadefoot suffers from habitat loss due to land conversion to livestock pasture and arable agriculture. Populations breeding in permanent ponds have already disappeared following predation of tadpoles by the invasive Eastern Mosquitofish (*Gambusia holbrooki*).

Identification Criteria
Similar to Western Spadefoot (page 54) but:
① Generally smaller
② Orange dots often present, especially on the eyelids

Size: 4–6cm
Habitat: Coastal plains, close to temporary ponds on uncultivated sandy soils with significant tree cover, usually in the form of open Cork Oak (*Quercus suber*) woodlands
Reproductive Period: October–January
Sexual Dimorphism: As for Western Spadefoot
Call: Similar to Western Spadefoot, but with higher-pitched notes
Spawn/Tadpoles: Generally similar to Western Spadefoot
IUCN Red List: Endangered

Left During the breeding season, males stay in the water and call day and night.

Right Tadpoles can overwinter and grow enormous.

Common Spadefoot – *Pelobates fuscus*

The Common Spadefoot is widespread in central and eastern Europe and has a varied appearance – it can be grey, brown or yellowish, with dark brown patches and usually orange dots. More active in humid weather, it is usually nocturnal, except during the breeding season, when it may also be diurnal. When threatened, it emits a distress call similar to that of the Western Spadefoot (page 54), but it also secretes a garlic-smelling toxin and can even jump towards its enemy to bite it. Although impressive, these behaviours are harmless to humans.

Identification Criteria
1. Pale blade, the same colour as the feet
2. Feet almost entirely webbed
3. Domed skull
4. Vertical pupil with a golden or orange iris

Size: 4–7cm
Habitat: Open, flat lowland areas with soft sandy soils or muddy and clay soils; can be found as far as 1km from water; breeds in shallow ponds or ditches with abundant vegetation, including rice fields; up to 700m
Reproductive Period: April–June
Sexual Dimorphism: As for Western Spadefoot; background coloration is often grey in females, muddy yellow in males
Call: Monotonous, muffled *dloak-dloak-dloak*, emitted underwater at night and also during the day
Spawn: Similar to Western Spadefoot but fewer eggs (<3,500 eggs)
Tadpoles: Generally similar to Western Spadefoot but tail longer, inter-eye distance shorter, and the tubercle of old tadpoles is pale; some tadpoles overwinter and, exceptionally, grow to 20cm
IUCN Red List: —

Left This species inhabits wetlands found across the flat Eastern European plains.

Right Colour patterns are very variable between individuals.

Pallas's Spadefoot – *Pelobates vespertinus*

Occurring in eastern Ukraine and Russia, Pallas's Spadefoot is often considered a subspecies of the Common Spadefoot (page 56), but genetic analysis supports its specific status. The two form a narrow contact zone, indicating reproductive isolation, and Pallas's Spadefoot has a significantly larger genome. Apart from their geographic distributions, which remain unclear in the north of its range, the two species are impossible to separate in the field.

Identification Criteria
Morphologically identical to Common Spadefoot and distinguishable only by distribution (see map)

Size: 4–7cm
Habitat: As for Common Spadefoot
Reproductive Period: April–June
Sexual Dimorphism: As for Common Spadefoot
Call: As for Common Spadefoot
Spawn/Tadpoles: As for Common Spadefoot
IUCN Red List: —

Left Spadefoot toads can bury themselves entirely in a few minutes.

Balkans Spadefoot – *Pelobates balcanicus*

Endemic to the region after which it was named, the Balkans Spadefoot is sympatric and sometimes syntopic with the Common Spadefoot (page 56) in Serbia and Romania, but can easily be distinguished by its flat skull (domed in Common) and partial feet webbing (more developed in Common). The tadpoles, however, cannot be separated. They can grow enormous, exceptionally up to 20cm, and so large that snakes sometimes choke to death while trying to eat them. The Balkans Spadefoot is usually considered a subspecies of the Eastern Spadefoot (page 59), but ongoing phylogenetic studies clearly indicate that the two are very different. A Peloponnese subspecies is also pending description.

Identification Criteria
1. Flat skull
2. Pale blade
3. Partial webbing of feet
4. Tiny warts on skin
5. Yellowish-red dots

Size: 5–9cm

Habitat: Similar to Common Spadefoot, but often in areas with less vegetation; up to 500m

Reproductive Period: March–May

Sexual Dimorphism: As for Western Spadefoot (page 54)

Call: Low-pitched *dloak-dloak-dloak*, emitted underwater all night long; more sonorous and louder than that of the Common Spadefoot and reminiscent of a tongue-clicking noise

Spawn/Tadpoles: Generally similar to Common Spadefoot

IUCN Red List: —

Right Specimens from the Levant, like this one, share similar morphologies and coloration with other populations, despite strong evolutionary divergence.

Eastern Spadefoot – *Pelobates syriacus*

The Eastern Spadefoot is limited to Anatolia, the Levant and the Caucasus, and has recently been separated from the Balkans Spadefoot (page 58), which occurs in the Balkans. This recent update has been the result of genetic analyses; morphological characterisation of these two species is pending further studies. Nowadays scattered in isolated patches, both the Eastern and Balkans spadefoots were widespread a few thousand years ago (and also present in north-eastern Europe), but experienced severe range contractions following global changes in climate.

Identification Criteria
Morphologically identical to Balkans Spadefoot and distinguishable only by distribution (see map)

Size: 5–9cm
Habitat: As for Balkans Spadefoot
Reproductive Period: March–May
Sexual Dimorphism: As for Western Spadefoot (page 54)
Call: As for Balkans Spadefoot
Spawn/Tadpoles: Probably similar to Common Spadefoot (page 56)
IUCN Red List: —

Above Males amplex females by the axillary position.

Above and right Metamorphs have rounded body forms (above). Males call with a vocal sac on the throat (right).

Hylidae

Hylidae is a richly varied family that is widespread in the Americas, Eurasia, North Africa and Australasia. Its members are commonly known as tree frogs due to their arboreal habits, their most obvious adaptation to this lifestyle being adhesive pads on the fingers and toes. More than 900 species in 55 genera have been described. A few of these have lost their taste for climbing; for instance, some *Cyclorana* frogs dig burrows and spend much of their lives underground, sometimes remaining dormant for more than five years, in order to survive drought conditions.

Only the genus *Hyla* occurs in the Western Palearctic, and includes nine distinct species. Eight of these are barely distinguishable without genetic tools and their distribution remains the sole reliable clue for identification in the field. With bodies that are small, slender and smooth, large eyes and characteristic climbing behaviour, these species are 'cute' frogs *par excellence*. They inhabit all kinds of shallow water bodies, preferring sunny, temporary ponds, and roost in the neighbouring vegetation (bushes and reeds) during the day. At night, male tree frogs gather together to form leks, chorusing very loudly in order to attract females. They hibernate in walls, under rocks or vegetation, or by burrowing into moist soil or a pile of leaves. Like chameleons, *Hyla* frogs can manipulate the tint of their skin colour (for example, from light to very dark green), either to match their environment and remain inconspicuous, or to enhance thermoregulation.

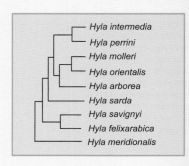

Hyla intermedia
Hyla perrini
Hyla molleri
Hyla orientalis
Hyla arborea
Hyla sarda
Hyla savignyi
Hyla felixarabica
Hyla meridionalis

Left Male tree frogs can sometimes call from outside the water.

Right *Hyla* tadpoles are incredibly fast swimmers.

European Tree Frog – *Hyla arborea*

Monitoring European Tree Frogs does not require you to get your boots wet: their powerful calls are heard from a long distance away and remain the best way to assess their presence. Locating a specimen will, however, require you to prospect the floating vegetation carefully, and eventually imitate its call so that it reveals its position by calling back. During the day, the frogs roost on nearby bushes. Historically, they were used as a kind of barometer, as they croak when rain is approaching. Individuals may be green, olive, brown or grey. The lateral line is extremely variable and can serve for individual recognition in capture–recapture studies.

Identification Criteria
① Horizontal pupil
② Tips of fingers and toes end in discs
③ Continuous black-and-white lateral line, ending in an inguinal loop
④ Smooth dorsal skin

Size: 3–5cm
Habitat: Shallow, sunny, temporary or permanent ponds and marshes in lowlands, usually with subaquatic vegetation; up to 2,300m
Reproductive Period: March–June
Sexual Dimorphism: Females are larger than males. Males have a yellowish vocal sac on the throat, which forms wrinkles at rest; females' throat is white and smooth
Call: Loud, rapid *peep-peep-peep-peep-peep-peep*; essentially nocturnal and heard in chorus
Spawn: Clutch of 200–1,000 eggs, deposited in clumps of 20–60 on vegetation
Tadpoles: Golden-olive coloration; <5cm; spiracle sinistral and slightly oriented upward; large lateral eyes; LTRF 2/3; very high upper tail fin, reaching as far as eyes; dark patches form a single line on the tail muscle; cloaca dextral; tail tip pointy; very fast swimmer
IUCN Red List: Least Concern

Left When disturbed during calling, the vocal sac of males deflates; they will eventually hide under the floating vegetation.

Italian Tree Frog – *Hyla intermedia*

Resembling other European tree frogs in coloration and voice, the Italian Tree Frog is nevertheless a valid distinct species. It is widely present in peninsular Italy south of the Apennines, and also occurs in Sicily. In central Italy, it meets and hybridises locally with the closely related Perrin's Tree Frog (page 63). As in other tree frogs, small males known as 'satellites' do not call but instead lurk near calling males to intercept the females they attract.

Identification Criteria
Morphologically identical to European Tree Frog (page 61) and distinguishable only by distribution (see map)

Size: 3–5cm
Habitat: As for European Tree Frog
Reproductive Period: March–May
Sexual Dimorphism: As for European Tree Frog
Call: As for European Tree Frog
Spawn/Tadpoles: As for European Tree Frog
IUCN Red List: —

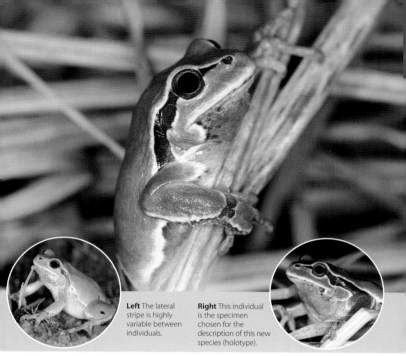

Left The lateral stripe is highly variable between individuals.

Right This individual is the specimen chosen for the description of this new species (holotype).

Perrin's Tree Frog – *Hyla perrini*

One of the most recent tree frog species to be discovered and described, Perrin's Tree Frog (or the Po Tree Frog) inhabits the Po Plain and adjacent north Italian valleys, as well as the Swiss canton of Ticino. My colleagues and I named it after my PhD adviser and friend, Professor Nicolas Perrin, as a tribute to his numerous scientific contributions in various fields of zoology, particularly regarding the evolution and diversity of Palearctic tree frogs. This species diverged several million years ago from its relatives the European Tree Frog (page 61) and Italian Tree Frog (page 62), with which it marginally admixes in north-eastern and central Italy respectively.

Identification Criteria
Morphologically identical to European Tree Frog and distinguishable only by distribution (see map)

Size: 3–5cm
Habitat: As for European Tree Frog
Reproductive Period: April–June
Sexual Dimorphism: As for European Tree Frog
Call: As for European Tree Frog
Spawn/Tadpoles: As for European Tree Frog
IUCN Red List: —

Left Tree frogs thermoregulate by changing their skin colour, and by carefully choosing their roosting place.

Iberian Tree Frog – *Hyla molleri*

The Iberian counterpart of the European Tree Frog (page 61), this species is actually more closely related to the Oriental Tree Frog (page 65). In south-western France, it widely hybridises with the European Tree Frog but not with the Mediterannean Tree Frog (page 69), which diverged much earlier. This species is not universally recognised yet and is waiting to receive a global conservation assessment.

Identification Criteria
Morphologically identical to European Tree Frog and distinguishable only by distribution (see map)

Size: 3–5cm
Habitat: As for European Tree Frog
Reproductive Period: March–June
Sexual Dimorphism: As for European Tree Frog
Call: As for European Tree Frog
Spawn/Tadpoles: As for European Tree Frog
IUCN Red List: —

Right Tree frogs are essentially nocturnal; they call by inflating and deflating a yellowish vocal sac.

Oriental Tree Frog – *Hyla orientalis*

Widespread in eastern Europe and Anatolia, the Oriental Tree Frog meets its European Tree Frog cousin (page 61) along the Carpathians and the Vistula River in Poland, which effectively act as natural barriers between the two species. Hybridisation is restricted anyway, however, perhaps because the frogs have evolved slightly different calls in the areas of contact – sufficient to avoid mating with one another, which would mean wasting their reproductive investments on unfit hybrid offspring. In Anatolia, it is unclear where the transition with the Middle East Tree Frog (page 67) is located, and the two might even be partially sympatric.

Identification Criteria
Morphologically identical to European Tree Frog and distinguishable only by distribution (see map)

Size: 3–5cm
Habitat: As for European Tree Frog
Reproductive Period: March–July
Sexual Dimorphism: As for European Tree Frog
Call: As for European Tree Frog
Spawn/Tadpoles: As for European Tree Frog
IUCN Red List: —

Left Tadpoles are a golden-olive colour with dark patches on the tail muscle.

Right Metamorphs progressively resorb their tail.

Tyrrhenian Tree Frog – *Hyla sarda*

This insular species is found on the Tyrrhenian islands of Corsica, Sardinia, Elbe and Capraia, which were formerly connected as the sea level was 120m lower during the last glaciation some 20,000 years ago. While its lifestyle is similar to that of continental hylids, the Tyrrhenian Tree Frog differs in a few visual features. It inhabits all kinds of natural and artificial water bodies, and is quite tolerant of heat – it can be found during the day sunbathing on rocks and dry walls. Unlike most of the other European *Hyla*, populations are relatively stable and the species is not threatened.

Identification Criteria
Similar to European Tree Frog (page 61) but:
① Inguinal loop absent
② Skin rougher than in other *Hyla*
③ Darker patches often present

Size: 3–5cm, usually smaller than European Tree Frog
Habitat: Different types of water bodies, including marshes, ponds, streams, ditches and water tanks
Reproductive Period: March–July
Sexual Dimorphism: As for European Tree Frog
Call: Similar to European Tree Frog but often slightly more rapid
Spawn/Tadpoles: Similar to European Tree Frog, but tadpoles have a shorter upper tail fin, reaching up to the spiracle
IUCN Red List: Least Concern

Left This species inhabits arid environments and can be found far away from water.

Right Amplexus can be formed on land.

Middle East Tree Frog – *Hyla savignyi*

This species is distributed from eastern Anatolia to Iran, and is also present on Cyprus. Its species name was given in recognition of the French zoologist Marie Jules de Savigny (1777–1851), who contributed to Napoleon's scientific expeditions in the eastern Mediterranean. The Middle East Tree Frog is generally smaller than European *Hyla* and differs in having an interrupted lateral line, forming spots, and in missing the inguinal loop. It lives in very hot, dry landscapes and is extremely resistant to heat and desiccation. The herpetologist may find it sitting on trees and bushes, sometimes far away from water bodies. The frogs reproduce in small permanent ponds, puddles and streams.

Identification Criteria
Similar to European Tree Frog (page 61) but:
① Interrupted lateral stripe, forming spots, and lacks the inguinal loop
② Coloration generally lighter (sometimes yellowish)

Size: 3–5cm, but generally smaller than European Tree Frog
Habitat: Steppes, deserts and semi-deserts, close to water bodies such as oases and garden ponds; up to 1,800m
Reproductive Period: January–June
Sexual Dimorphism: As for European Tree Frog
Call: Similar to European Tree Frog but the notes are better defined and higher pitched, *pep-pep-pep-pep*, and emitted at a slower pace (~3 per second); reminiscent of a duck's quacking, with large choruses sounding like cicadas
Spawn/Tadpoles: Generally similar to European Tree Frog
IUCN Red List: Least Concern

Left The snout profile in this species appears truncated.

Right The subtle inguinal loop may sometimes be missing.

Arabian Tree Frog – *Hyla felixarabica*

This is a new species recently described from Yemen. Its species epithet, *felixarabica*, means 'fruitful Arabia' and was the name given by ancient geographers to the southern Arabian Peninsula. Closely related to the Middle East Tree Frog (page 67), it differs from that species genetically as well as in some subtle acoustic and morphological features. Some individuals have a pale beige colour phase. The distribution of the Arabian Tree Frog is disjointed: it is mainly present in Saudi Arabia and Yemen, but isolated populations also persist in the Levant region, some 1,000km north, where it meets and hybridises with the Middle East Tree Frog.

Identification Criteria
Similar to Middle East Tree Frog but:
(1) Small inguinal loop usually present
(2) Snout profile usually truncated (rounder in Middle East Tree Frog)

Size: 3–5cm
Habitat: Springs and all types of small waterholes, including artificial ponds in desert regions
Reproductive Period: December–February, but can be prolonged depending on rainfall
Sexual Dimorphism: As for European Tree Frog (page 61)
Call: Similar to Middle East Tree Frog, but notes are shorter, more widely spaced and slightly higher pitched
Spawn/Tadpoles: Generally similar to European Tree Frog
IUCN Red List: —

Left Tadpoles of this species are more pigmented than other tree frogs.

Right Metamorphs and juveniles can display a black lateral line.

Mediterranean Tree Frog – *Hyla meridionalis*

Native to North Africa and Iberia, the Mediterranean Tree Frog might also be found hopping off your salad – it has been known to travel hundreds of kilometres hidden among fruits and vegetables exported from these regions. This travelling habit dates back to antiquity: the Catalonian, French, Italian, and even Canary and Balearic populations originate from old translocations from North Africa by ancient civilisations. The species is easily separable from other tree frogs by its lack of a lateral line and its very different, low-pitched call – in fact, it used to be called *Hyla barytomus* in recognition of the latter feature.

Identification Criteria
Similar to European Tree Frog (page 61) but:
① Black-and-white lateral line does not extend further than the shoulder
② Generally larger

Size: 3–7cm
Habitat: Different kinds of permanent or temporary, calm water bodies in lowlands, usually with vegetation; often associated with settlements (for example, orchards and irrigation ditches); up to 1,000m
Reproductive Period: April–June, usually starting a bit later than other European *Hyla*
Sexual Dimorphism: As for European Tree Frog
Call: Slow, low-pitched, grumpy-sounding *kroaaak… kroaaak… kroaaak* croaks (1 note per second or less)
Spawn: Similar to other *Hyla*, but deposited in smaller clumps (10–30 eggs each)
Tadpoles: Similar to European Tree Frog, but the upper tail fin is generally shorter, reaching only up to the spiracle; has two or three dark lines on the tail muscles; LTRF 2/3, but second upper tooth row is largely incomplete
IUCN Red List: Least Concern

Bufonidae

The Latin word *bufo* simply means 'toad', and members of the Bufonidae family are accordingly known as true toads. It is a very large family, with more than 35 genera and 500 species, and is widespread on every continent except Australia and Antarctica. The species inhabit all kinds of environments, from deserts to snowy mountains and rainforests. Almost all bufonids lay eggs in strings, these hatching into tadpoles. One genus from Tanzania (*Nectophrynoides*), however, is ovoviviparous, meaning that fertilisation is internal and the larvae develop within the female, which gives birth to fully developed toadlets. Bufonids move by crawling and running, rather than hopping like frogs do, and are particularly mobile, especially during spring migrations.

In addition to their horizontal pupil and warty skin, bufonids are characterised by having a pair of parotoid glands on the back of their head, which contains an alkaloid poison that is discharged under stress. The particular type of toxin produced depends on the species, but collectively they are known under the

Top Toads, such as these *Bufo spinosus*, form axillary amplexus, where the female walks and swims with the male until she lays her eggs.

Above Worms form part of the diet of bufonids, including the Natterjack Toad, and are easier to catch after a long period of rain.

general term bufotoxins. The notorious Cane Toad (*Rhinella marina*), an invasive species in Australia, is extremely poisonous, and its ingestion can kill a crocodile. Other bufonids can paralyse or kill dogs, and raccoons and birds have learnt how to eat them while avoiding the poison glands. The bufotoxins produced by some species can be powerfully psychoactive and are used as hallucinogenic drugs for recreational purposes. Bufonid tadpoles

Left Green toads, such as this European Green Toad, feature colourful camouflage, allowing them to remain unnoticed in gravel and rocky environments.

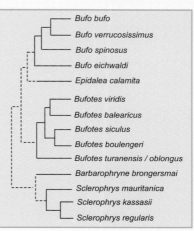

Right In more arid areas, the camouflage of the Berber Toad features sandy colours.

also exude toxins to deter predation by fishes.

Across the Western Palearctic, the diversity of bufonids is relatively poor, with only five genera and at least 14 species. Two of the genera have radiated and diversified across the region, each now forming a group of closely related species that are hard to separate: the *Bufo bufo* complex (four species) and the *Bufotes viridis* complex (four species, excluding Asian relatives). A third includes only one species, the Natterjack Toad (*Epidalea calamita*), while the last two are North African representatives, *Sclerophrys* (three species) and *Barbarophryne* (one species).

Bufo bufo
Bufo verrucosissimus
Bufo spinosus
Bufo eichwaldi
Epidalea calamita
Bufotes viridis
Bufotes balearicus
Bufotes siculus
Bufotes boulengeri
Bufotes turanensis / oblongus
Barbarophryne brongersmai
Sclerophrys mauritanica
Sclerophrys kassasii
Sclerophrys regularis

Left The colour of *Bufo bufo* allows it to remain hidden; this is not the case for its egg strings.

Right Black tadpoles swarming in ponds during spring are usually Common Toads.

Common Toad – *Bufo bufo*

Widespread, from seashores to mountaintops, Common Toads wait for a good downfall of rain before migrating by the thousands towards suitable breeding sites, a journey during which the toads can be decimated by road traffic. Cold-adapted, the species breeds very early, sometimes even before thaw in high-altitude populations. Males are extremely aggressive and many try mating simultaneously with the same female, which may die in the process. The toads are sometimes infected by parasitic flies (*Lucilia* and *Bufolucilia* spp.), whose larvae eat into the flesh of adults. A bivalve, the European Fingernail Clam (*Sphaerium corneum*), uses the toad as transport by climbing on its toes.

Identification Criteria
1. Grey, brown or rufous coloration
2. Yellow iris (in the north) and horizontal pupil
3. Prominent, roughly parallel parotoid glands (in the north)
4. Metatarsal tubercle small and round (in the north)
5. More similar to Spiny Toad (page 73) in southern parts of the range

Size: 7–15cm

Habitat: Cosmopolitan, provided large, sunny and relatively deep ponds are available; up to 2,200m

Reproductive Period: January–June

Sexual Dimorphism: Females are bigger and more colourful than males; males have nuptial calluses on the first fingers of the forefeet

Call: Weak, slow, rough *coaerk… coaerk… coaerk…* release calls, faster (2–3 per second) and more metallic, are more easily heard

Spawn: Up to 8,000 eggs deposited in two cords 3–5m long, stretched around vegetation

Tadpoles: Black with a dark fin; <4cm; spiracle sinistral and horizontal; inter-eye distance = mouth width = 2× inter-nostril distance; LTRF 2/3; occurs in swarms, usually close to the water's surface

IUCN Red List: —

Left Toad spawn is arranged in cords, stretched around objects in the water.

Right The skin of the Spiny Toad is covered in thorny warts.

Spiny Toad – *Bufo spinosus*

The Spiny Toad is the North African/Iberian counterpart of the Common Toad (page 72), with which it hybridises across central France. In western Europe it is distinguished from that species by its much bigger size, thorny warts (hence its name) and intensely red iris. However, the '*spinosus*' morphotype has also evolved independently in southern Common Toad populations in the Balkans, and may thus be an adaptation to the dry Mediterranean climate. Hence, the criteria above can be used to distinguish the Common Toad from the Spiny Toad only in their parapatric ranges. Despite its abundance, the Spiny Toad is declining, particularly in the most arid areas of Spain.

Identification Criteria
Similar to Common Toad but:
1. Much larger in size, especially females
2. Intense red iris
3. Thorny warts with a keratinised tip, especially near the mouth and parotoid glands
4. Parotoid glands not parallel, but V-shaped
5. Metatarsal tubercle large and narrow

Size: 7–18cm
Habitat: As for Common Toad; up to 2,500m
Reproductive Period: January–May
Sexual Dimorphism: As for Common Toad; females usually have coloured motifs (dark/light camouflage patterns)
Call: As for Common Toad
Spawn: As for Common Toad
Tadpoles: Similar to Common Toad but metamorphs are yellowish red; smaller in North Africa (<3cm)
IUCN Red List: —

Left This species breeds in all kinds of puddles, ponds, brooks and springs.

Right Like other *Bufo* species, eggs are laid in strings of, usually, two rows.

Caucasian Toad – *Bufo verrucosissimus*

The Caucasian Toad has a highly fragmented distribution in the mountain forests of the Caucasus. It is very similar to the Common Toad (page 72); the ranges of the two species meet in Turkey. The species breeds mostly in clear, flowing waters, such as brooks or springs, but it can also be found in puddles and ponds. Sexual dimorphism is more pronounced than in the other species of the *Bufo bufo* complex, supposedly so that the large females can carry their small male mating partners for a long period of time in order to search for a suitable breeding site. Like many Caucasian amphibians, this species is threatened by predation by invasive Raccoons (*Procyon lotor*).

Identification Criteria
Similar to Common Toad but:
① Uniform, dull brownish-grey coloration
② Black stripes on the parotoid glands (not reaching the tympanum)
③ Generally bigger

Size: 7–19cm
Habitat: Coniferous and deciduous mountain forests; breeding sites are usually shared and include brooks, rivers and puddles, as well as permanent water bodies; up to 1,900m
Reproductive Period: February–August
Sexual Dimorphism: Similar to Common Toad but much more pronounced, with males being much smaller than females. Coloration is the same in both sexes
Call: As for Common Toad
Spawn/Tadpoles: As for Common Toad
IUCN Red List: Near Threatened

Left The black marking on parotoids can vary between individuals.

Eichwald's Toad – *Bufo eichwaldi*

Also known as the Talysh Toad, this was formerly considered a subspecies of the Caucasian Toad (page 74), which it closely resembles. The ecology of the species has been poorly studied and its exclusively nocturnal habits make it difficult to observe. It is rare in most of its highly fragmented range and is threatened by deforestation, and potentially by the invasive Raccoon (*Procyon lotor*) and Eastern Mosquitofish (*Gambusia holbrooki*), which prey heavily on adults and larvae respectively. These threats have resulted in a decline in numbers of more than 30 per cent over the last three decades.

Identification Criteria
Similar to Caucasian Toad but:
1. Abrupt snout tip (rounded in Caucasian Toad)
2. Parotoid gland markings reach the tympanum
3. Dark spots on back and belly in males

Size: 8–17cm
Habitat: Mainly deciduous mountain forests at low altitude, but sometimes lowland swamps, gardens and plantations; breeds in mountain springs; up to 1,200m
Reproductive Period: March–June
Sexual Dimorphism: Similar to Caucasian Toad but males have dark spots on the belly
Call: As for Common Toad (page 72)
Spawn/Tadpoles: As for Common Toad
IUCN Red List: Vulnerable

Left *Bufotes* mating calls can be compared to the shrill sound of some crickets.

Right The eastern subspecies *B. v. variabilis* (seen here) is called the Variable Green Toad.

European Green Toad – *Bufotes viridis*

One of the region's most beautiful anurans, the European Green Toad is more frequently heard than seen. Its vibrating whistle can be confused with other wet meadow residents like the Mole Cricket (*Gryllotalpa gryllotalpa*) or the Whimbrel (*Numenius phaeopus*). The toad is quite tolerant of heat, desiccation and salinity, and can be found in estuaries. Although abundant in southern parts of its range, the European Green Toad is disappearing in northern and western areas due to habitat destruction and urbanisation. Despite this, it commonly occurs in anthropogenic habitats, including cities, living in industrial waste ponds and eating flying insects attracted by street lighting.

Identification Criteria
① Horizontal pupil and citrus-green iris
② Green patches on pale background
③ Parotoid glands nearly parallel

Size: 7–10cm
Habitat: Dry, open areas like steppes and meadows with shallow water; often close to human settlements; up to 2,400m
Reproductive Period: February–June
Sexual Dimorphism: Females are larger than males and have more contrasting and colourful camouflage patterns. Breeding males have a vocal sac on the throat and nuptial calluses on the first fingers of the forefeet
Call: Vibrating, melodic *eeerrrrrr* trill lasting ~10 seconds, emitted at night by males standing on the shore or on aquatic vegetation
Spawn: Lays 1–2 strings, each 2–4m long, on the floor or vegetation
Tadpoles: Dark brown or grey/greenish with a clear fin; <5cm; variable presence of dark spots on the tail; fin asymmetric – upper tail fin higher than lower tail fin; spiracle sinistral and horizontal; inter-eye distance ≥ mouth width = 1.5× inter-nostril distance; LTRF 2/3
Subspecies: Two (page 195)
IUCN Red List: Least Concern

Left Note the coloured spots on the parotoid glands.

Right Fresh clutches can be found in sandy rainwater puddles.

Balearic Green Toad – *Bufotes balearicus*

A lowland species, the Balearic Green Toad is widespread in continental Italy, and common in Corsica and Sardinia. As its name implies, it also occurs in the Balearic Islands, where it was probably introduced during the Bronze Age. Its specific status is supported by its restricted hybridisation with the European Green Toad (page 76) in north-eastern Italy and the absence of hybridisation with the Sicilian Green Toad (page 78) in Sicily. Typical of sand dunes, the species is also widely present in cultivated and urban areas, and often wanders near human settlements. It is declining as a result of increased agrochemical pollutants and urbanisation, and is extinct in Switzerland despite reintroduction efforts.

Identification Criteria
Similar to European Green Toad but:
① Red or brownish spots on parotoid glands
② Often has reddish-orange coloration

Size: 7–10cm
Habitat: Coastal areas such as sand dunes, as well as cultivated and urban areas, including meadows, ponds, and gravel and sand pits; up to 1,300m
Reproductive Period: February–April
Sexual Dimorphism: As for European Green Toad
Call: As for European Green Toad
Spawn/Tadpoles: As for European Green Toad
IUCN Red List: Least Concern

Left This species is adapted to the very dry Sicilian landscape.

Sicilian Green Toad – *Bufotes siculus*

This Sicilian endemic remained unnoticed until it was described in 2008, when researchers realised it belonged to a distinct genetic lineage, more closely related to the African Green Toad (page 79) than the European Green Toad (page 76) and Balearic Green Toad (page 77). It displays strong colour variation but can be differentiated from the neighbouring Balearic Green Toad by a few features. Its breeding period is also longer, as it may potentially reproduce twice during the year.

Identification Criteria
Similar to Balearic Green Toad but:
① No coloured spots on parotoid glands
② No reddish-orange coloration

Size: 7–10cm
Habitat: As for Balearic Green Toad; up to 1,200m
Reproductive Period: January–June and September–November
Sexual Dimorphism: As for European Green Toad
Call: As for European Green Toad
Spawn/Tadpoles: As for European Green Toad
IUCN Red List: Least Concern

Left The size and patterns of the green camouflage can vary greatly between individuals.

Right Like other toads, *Bufotes boulengeri* lays egg strings in very shallow, temporary waters.

African Green Toad – *Bufotes boulengeri*

Widespread in North Africa, from Western Sahara to Egypt, this species occurs in fragmented populations in desert wetlands and oases. Its range may be further extended to Saudi Arabia, Yemen, Israel and Jordan pending genetic identification of those populations, and it is also present on the island of Lampedusa in Italy. Not much is known about the ecology and population trends of the species. It is assumed that it is suffering loss of its breeding habitats via wetland drainage and drought; industrial and agricultural pollution may also be a threat locally.

Identification Criteria
Similar to Sicilian Green Toad (page 78) but:
(1) Variable presence of a dorsal stripe

Size: 7–10cm
Habitat: Arid, open landscapes, from coasts to mountain plateaux; breeds in temporary ponds
Reproductive Period: January–May
Sexual Dimorphism: As for European Green Toad (page 76)
Call: As for European Green Toad
Spawn/Tadpoles: Similar to European Green Toad, but tadpoles can be larger (up to 6cm)
IUCN Red List: Least Concern

Left With their sandy-coloured military camouflage, these green toads cannot be confused with other species.

Central Asian Green Toads – *Bufotes turanensis/oblongus* complex

G reen toads of Asian origin can be found at the very eastern edge of the Western Palearctic. Northern Iran and Turkmenistan are inhabited by a complex of species with different levels of ploidy (the number of copies of each chromosome): the diploid *Bufotes 'turanensis'* (two chromosomal copies) and the tetraploid *B. oblongus* (four chromosomal copies), as well as their triploid hybrids (three chromosomal copies). According to current distribution data, only *B. 'turanensis'* reaches our area, on the south-eastern shores of the Caspian Sea. The taxonomy of these species will be updated following recent research, especially for *B. 'turanensis'*, which has distinct evolutionary lineages throughout central Asia.

Identification Criteria
Morphologically identical to European Green Toad (page 76) and distinguishable only by distribution (see map)

Size: 7–10cm
Habitat: Arid mountains and hilly deserts, with slow-moving streams and ponds for breeding
Reproductive Period: April–June
Sexual Dimorphism: As for European Green Toad
Call: As for European Green Toad
Spawn/Tadpoles: As for European Green Toad
IUCN Red List: Least Concern

Left This species breeds in shallow waters without vegetation, such as in gravel pits.

Right Tadpoles do not aggregate together as they do in *Bufo bufo*.

Natterjack Toad – *Epidalea calamita*

A distant cousin of the green toads inhabiting western Europe, the Natterjack Toad is usually found in shallow, temporarily flooded areas that are well exposed to the sun. It is a runner rather than a jumper, and can move as fast as a mouse. Its main predators are birds, including owls and gulls; spiders can prey on tadpoles and metamorphs. In northern and eastern parts of the species' range, numbers have drastically declined in past decades. It has been studied in detail in Britain, where it has been the subject of reintroduction efforts. In winter, the toad burrows near reproductive sites. Hybrids with the European Green Toad (page 76) have been locally reported in Germany and Sweden.

Identification Criteria
1. Yellow dorsal line
2. Iris bright yellow or greenish, pupil black and shaped like a horizontal ellipse
3. Parotoid glands parallel
4. Warts often reddish in colour
5. Stocky build, with short hindlimbs

Size: 5–9cm
Habitat: Shallow, temporary water bodies in sunny, open habitats with sparse vegetation and loose soils, such as alluvial zones, gravel pits and flooded meadows; up to 2,400m
Reproductive Period: January–August
Sexual Dimorphism: Females are larger than males; males have dark nuptial calluses, a large sub-gular vocal sac and a blue throat (throat is off-white in females)
Call: Loud metallic trills, errrp… errrp… errrp…, each lasting 1–2 seconds, are made at night; can be heard up to 2km away; may potentially be confused with a Nightjar (*Caprimulgus europaeus*)
Spawn: Deposits 1–2 strings of eggs, each 1–2m long (2,000–7,000 eggs in total), directly on the pond floor (depth <20cm)
Tadpoles: Usually scattered. Black with dark fins and a white gular spot; <4cm; LTRF 2/3; spiracle sinistral and horizontal; inter-eye distance = 2× mouth width = 2× inter-nostril distance
IUCN Red List: Least Concern

Left Growth rate and body size vary greatly, due to the conditions of its arid habitat.

Right Note the smooth and rounded parotoid glands.

Moroccan Green Toad – *Barbarophryne brongersmai*

This Moroccan endemic inhabits rocky areas in the hills of the western Sahara. Reproduction is explosive, taking place in a small temporal window: the toads wait for incidental spring showers, and breed in temporary puddles, streams and ponds. The species may also use artificial water bodies like irrigation ditches or dammed rivers. It is decreasing due to destruction of its breeding sites and increasing aridity in its range, and is consequently listed as Near Threatened by the IUCN. It is sympatric (but not necessarily syntopic) with the African Green Toad (page 79), but adults cannot be confused owing to their different size, shape, coloration and mating call. Reliable field identification of tadpoles is, however, very difficult.

Identification Criteria
1. Elongated, slender appearance
2. Absence of warts on the dorsal head surface
3. Almost round parotoid glands
4. Spotted belly (unspotted in African Green Toad)

Size: 4–5cm
Habitat: Semi-arid hilly areas; up to 1,600m
Reproductive Period: February–April
Sexual Dimorphism: Females are larger than males; breeding males have a gular vocal sac and hand calluses
Call: Short, squeaky pulses, each lasting 1–2 seconds
Spawn: Two strings with low egg density are deposited on the ground or between stones and branches
Tadpoles: Generally similar to African Green Toad but tail fins are unspotted and usually not asymmetric
IUCN Red List: Near Threatened

Left The intense red colour of some individuals mimics the sandy deserts they inhabit.

Right The tadpole of the Berber Toad can be distinguished from others by its marbled golden colour.

Berber Toad – *Sclerophrys mauritanica*

A large toad with very variably coloured patches, spanning the entire red spectrum (from dark brown to orange), on a sandy or olive base; the patches may be absent or cover the entire back. The species' North African distribution is very fragmented; a population was also introduced near Los Alcornocales Natural Park in southern Spain in the early twentieth century. It inhabits a wide array of habitats, from coastal dunes to rocky mountain areas, and breeds in fresh or brackish water. Crepuscular and nocturnal, the Berber Toad hunts various insects and even scorpions. It can be found at high altitudes in the Atlas Mountains.

Identification Criteria
① Large brown, red or orange patches
② Marked tympanum
③ Roughly parallel, kidney-shaped parotoid glands

Size: 7–15cm
Habitat: Subtropical or tropical dry Cork Oak (*Quercus suber*) forests, shrubland, rivers, marshes, arable or pasture land, plantations and urban areas; up to 2,600m
Reproductive Period: February–June; can breed several times per year, but can also skip a year due to drought
Sexual Dimorphism: Females are bigger than males and usually more colourful; males have nuptial calluses on the first fingers of the forefeet during breeding
Call: Fast, low, progressive *ro-ro-ro-ro-ro-ro-roaarrr*, emitted in a short series
Spawn: 5,000–10,000 eggs deposited in strings
Tadpoles: Small (<3cm); body black with tiny golden spots; fin dark grey, long and narrow, ending at the base of the tail; spiracle sinistral; LTRF 2/3
IUCN Red List: Least Concern

Left Unlike females, males have colourful throats.

Nile Valley Toad – *Sclerophrys kassasii*

The range of the small Nile Valley Toad is apparent in its common name: it is endemic to the Egyptian wetlands and croplands along the Nile River and in its delta. Mostly aquatic, it is related to other tropical African species in the genus: before 1993, it was confused with *Sclerophrys vittata*, a relative from Uganda. The Nile Valley Toad is relatively abundant in swamps and rice fields, and has spread as far upstream as Luxor, following the reeds that overgrow the banks of the Nile River and its canals. It is also found in urban areas, including Cairo. It is easily heard, but its small size and the dense vegetation of its habitat make it hard to spot.

Identification Criteria
① Large, distinct tympanum
② Indistinct parotoid glands
③ Granular, spiny back

Size: 3–4cm
Habitat: Swamps and rice fields in the Nile Valley and delta
Reproductive Period: Potentially all year round, especially spring and autumn
Sexual Dimorphism: Males have yellow or orange throats
Call: Short, sharp rattle-like trills *rrrrii-rrriii-rrrii* (1–2 trills per second); can be heard day and night
Spawn/Tadpoles: Not substantially described, supposedly similar to other *Sclerophrys*; small clutches (300 eggs) were observed in captivity
IUCN Red List: Least Concern

Right This toad is a dark olive-brown colour with dark patches that probably evolved for camouflage.

African Common Toad – *Sclerophrys regularis*

Widespread throughout sub-Saharan Africa, this amphibian occurs naturally in the Western Palearctic only, along the Nile River and in its delta, where it is abundant. It has been introduced to the Sinai Peninsula, and has also been exported in large numbers to Canada as part of the international pet trade. The species has several alternative names, including Square-marked Toad, Egyptian Toad and Bouncing Toad (the latter refers to the bouncing motion of the toad as it tries to confuse or escape from predators).

Identification Criteria
1. Large tympanum with a shallow depression
2. Prominent parallel parotoid glands
3. Dark olive-brown coloration with dark patches

Size: 6–13cm
Habitat: Within the region covered, it inhabits the swampy banks of the Nile River and delta
Reproductive Period: Opportunistic breeder, can be heard all year long
Sexual Dimorphism: Females are larger than males; males have black throats and nuptial calluses on their first fingers during the breeding period
Call: Lengthy rattling trills, rrrroaaarrrr… rrrroaaarrrr… rrrroaaarrrr, each lasting ~1 second
Spawn: 10,000 eggs deposited in double strings
Tadpoles: Dark brown body with a white-spotted tail; <3cm; spiracle sinistral; does not aggregate
IUCN Red List: Least Concern

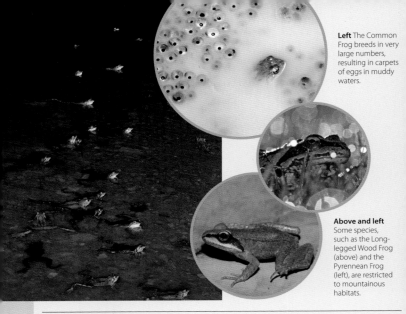

Left The Common Frog breeds in very large numbers, resulting in carpets of eggs in muddy waters.

Above and left Some species, such as the Long-legged Wood Frog (above) and the Pyrennean Frog (left), are restricted to mountainous habitats.

Ranidae – Genus *Rana*

Ranidae, or true frogs, is one of the largest amphibian families, and one of the most controversial in taxonomic terms. Species are abundant throughout all continents (except Antarctica), and are usually characterised by a moist, smooth skin and slender, webbed legs that have evolved for hopping and swimming. They include the largest amphibian on Earth, the Goliath Frog (*Conraua goliath*), which reaches 32cm in length. In the Western Palearctic, there are only two native genera of ranid frogs: the brown frogs (*Rana*) and the water frogs (*Pelophylax*).

Rana, or brown frogs, are widespread throughout Eurasia and North America. While the taxonomic position of many species is disputed, current lists account for at least 50 species worldwide. In Europe, they are all brownish, with a black temporal mark. They spawn eggs in gelatinous clumps of various sizes, usually early in the season, when males emit discreet mating calls via internal vocal sacs. We can consider two groups: the widespread Common Frog (*Rana temporaria*), Moor Frog (*R. arvalis*) and Agile Frog (*R. dalmatina*);

and the more localised Italian Agile Frog (*R. latastei*; southern Alps), Italian Stream Frog (*R. italica*; Apennine Peninsula), Greek Stream Frog (*R. graeca*; southern Balkans), Iberian Frog (*R. iberica*, Iberia) and Pyrenean Frog (*R. pyrenaica*; Pyrenees). The region extending from Anatolia to the Middle East is inhabited by a different set of species represented by the Long-legged Wood Frog (*R. macrocnemis*), Tavas Frog (*R. tavasensis*) and Hyrcanian Frog (*R. pseudodalmatina*). Several species are sympatric and identification requires careful inspection of leg size, head shape and colour patterns.

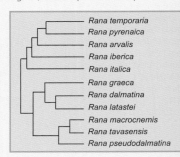

Rana temporaria
Rana pyrenaica
Rana arvalis
Rana iberica
Rana italica
Rana graeca
Rana dalmatina
Rana latastei
Rana macrocnemis
Rana tavasensis
Rana pseudodalmatina

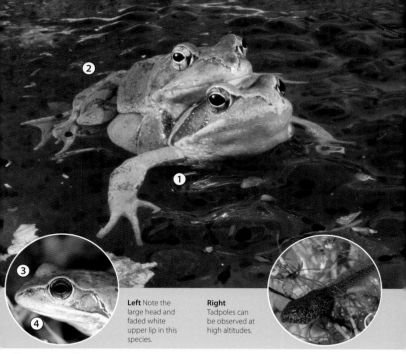

Left Note the large head and faded white upper lip in this species.

Right Tadpoles can be observed at high altitudes.

Common Frog – *Rana temporaria*

Widespread, abundant and ubiquitous, the Common Frog is called common for a reason. Yet the herpetologist will have to wear warm clothes and go into the field early in spring to enjoy seeing it, since it is one of our most precocious species. While usually brownish, it can actually be found in a variety of colours, from yellow to black. Despite its resemblance to other brown frogs sharing its vast distribution range, the Common Frog does not hybridise and should not be confused with them. In north-western Spain, the subspecies *Rana temporaria parvipalmata* (page 196) might soon be raised to full species level.

Identification Criteria
1. Slender brown frog with a horizontal pupil and dark temporal markings
2. Short hindlimbs (leg test: not reaching the snout)
3. Large head and truncated snout, with tympanum far away from, and smaller than, the eyes
4. Faded white upper lip
5. Small, smooth metatarsal tubercle

Size: 7–10cm
Habitat: Terrestrial, breeding in a broad range of fresh waters from coasts to mountains; up to 3,000m
Reproductive Period: Explosive breeding during a short window of a few weeks from February–June
Sexual Dimorphism: Males have dark nuptial pads on the first fingers
Call: Discreet, rumbling rrroooak… rrroooak… rrroooak…, reminiscent of a distant motorcycle; can be heard day and night
Spawn: Eggs large (1cm with capsule); deposited in clusters of 700–4,500 eggs in the water, often forming giant gelatinous masses
Tadpoles: Small (<4.5cm); brown/dark with white/golden pigmentation; spiracle sinistral, diagonally oriented upward; cloaca dextral; low upper tail fin and tail tip curvy; LTRF 3–4/4
Subspecies: Two (page 196)
IUCN Red List: Least Concern

Left Individuals often display a pale stripe on the back.

Moor Frog – *Rana arvalis*

This is a central and eastern European species whose range extends as far east as the Altai Mountains in Asia. Moor Frogs inhabit diverse open lowland habitats, and usually drier sites than the Common Frog (page 87), from which they differ in a few features. During a few days in spring, breeding males display an impressive blue coloration. The species is generally not under threat except in its periphery, where populations can become isolated. In central Europe, a larger subspecies, *Rana arvalis wolterstorfii* (page 197), is present, which has longer legs and a slender appearance.

Identification Criteria
1. Short hindlimbs (leg test: barely reaching the snout)
2. Head more tapered than in Common Frog, with a pointy snout
3. Pale vertebral band generally present (generally absent in Common Frog)
4. Metatarsal tubercle large and hard

Size: 5–8cm
Habitat: Lowland open swamps, steppes, tundra, meadows and forest edges; up to 800m
Reproductive Period: March–June
Sexual Dimorphism: As for Common Frog, plus males have a blue coloration during the breeding season
Call: Sudden, muffled *woag… woag… woag*, reminiscent of bubbles escaping from a bottle underwater or a small dog barking
Spawn: Similar to Common Frog, although usually deposited on aquatic vegetation
Tadpoles: Generally similar to Common Frog, but LTRF 2–3/3 and tail tip pointy
Subspecies: Two (page 197)
IUCN Red List: Least Concern

Left Tadpoles are among the most colourful found in European anurans.

Right Agile Frogs have much longer forelimbs than similar species.

Agile Frog – *Rana dalmatina*

The slender Agile Frog inhabits deciduous forests and is potentially found together with most other European brown frogs. However, it has much longer hindlimbs than the Common Frog (page 87) and Moor Frog (page 88), and can be distinguished from Italian Agile Frog (page 90), Italian Stream Frog (page 91), Greek Stream Frog (page 92) and Iberian Frog (page 93) by the size and position of its tympanum, as well as the colour patterns on its white upper lip and throat. Apart from those in southern Italy, most Agile Frog populations are genetically uniform, suggesting that the species recolonised Europe from a few sources after the last ice age. Its long legs allow amazingly extended jumps, up to 2m in distance.

Identification Criteria
1. Long hindlimbs (leg test: largely exceeding the snout)
2. Tympanum prominent, very close to the eye (1–2mm) and of similar diameter
3. Very pointy snout and narrow, flattened head
4. White upper lip ending towards snout
5. Pale throat, sometimes mottled on side only

Size: 4–8cm
Habitat: Deciduous forests with various types of still water bodies nearby; up to 1,700m
Reproductive Period: February–May
Sexual Dimorphism: Similar to Common Frog, but nuptial calluses are greyish
Call: Series of fast *cog-cog-cog-cog-cog-cog-cog* notes (4–6 notes per second), reaching a crescendo
Spawn: Similar to Common Frog, but usually deposits smaller clumps (<2,000 eggs) around aquatic shoots or branches; the clumps later surface, covered with algae
Tadpoles: Generally similar to Common Frog, <6cm; but light brown or rufous in colour; higher upper tail fin with pointy tail tip; dark protuberance on the upper beak
IUCN Red List: Least Concern

Left Examining the throat is a useful way of identifying this species.

Right In Italy, the interrupted white lip is specific to this species.

Italian Agile Frog – *Rana latastei*

Restricted to the Po Plain and adjacent valleys, the Italian Agile Frog is a lowland species inhabiting moist, partially flooded forest areas. Its species epithet is in honour of Fernand Lataste (1847–1934), a famous French herpetologist who described several species in the late nineteenth century. This small frog 'miaows' to attract females. Morphologically similar to the sympatric Agile Frog (page 89), it differs in some specific colour features (throat and upper lip). The species is the prey of crows as well as forest mammals like Weasels (*Mustela nivalis*), Badgers (*Meles meles*) and Pine Martens (*Martes martes*), and even Hedgehogs (*Erinaceus europaeus*) and voles.

Identification Criteria

1. Long hindlimbs (leg test: largely exceeding the snout)
2. Discreet tympanum, far away from, and much smaller than, the eye
3. Dark throat with a central pale line
4. White upper lip, ending abruptly under the eye
5. Between-nostrils distance < eye–nostril distance
6. Legs and groin sometimes reddish

Size: 4–6cm
Habitat: Lowland areas, in very humid, partially flooded forests, with swampy soil and dense ground vegetation; up to 500m
Reproductive Period: February–April
Sexual Dimorphism: Breeding males have dark brown calluses on the thumbs, and rufous spots on the throat and groin
Call: Slow, prolonged, smooth *Meowwwww*, like a cat's miaow, emitted underwater; long intervals between calls (up to 1 minute); can be heard day and night
Spawn: Eggs small (6–7mm with capsule); deposited in small clusters (300–400 eggs) and fixed around branches or on aquatic vegetation
Tadpoles: Similar to Agile Frog but more brownish, and with strong tail pigmentation and no dark protuberance on the beak
IUCN Red List: Vulnerable

Right This species is
more stockily built than the
slender *Rana latastei* and
R. dalmatina.

Italian Stream Frog – *Rana italica*

This Italian endemic is very
similar to the Greek Stream
Frog (page 92); it was formerly
considered conspecific with
(before 1985), and then a
subspecies (1985–90) of that
species. Fortunately, the two
have distinct distribution ranges
and thus cannot be confused.
In its natural habitat, the Italian
Stream Frog can potentially be
mistaken only for the Agile Frog
(page 89), which has a pale throat
and a different tympanum, and
the Italian Agile Frog (page 90) in
the Po Plain, whose nostrils are
closer together. Egg clutches are
deposited under stones on the
riverbed and males can guard the
site for a short period of time.

Identification Criteria

1. Small, stocky body with long
   hindlimbs
2. Short, round snout
3. Discreet tympanum, far away
   from the eye and of much
   smaller diameter
4. Black throat with a white
   median line
5. Between-nostrils distance >
   eye–nostril distance

Size: 4–6cm
Habitat: Mountain streams with
rocky beds; up to 1,700m
Reproductive Period: February–April
Sexual Dimorphism: Males have dark nuptial calluses during
breeding, these becoming lighter outside the breeding period
Call: Low-pitched, fast *gek-gek-gek-gek-gek*; mostly nocturnal
Spawn: Deposits grape-like clusters of 600–800 eggs under stones
Tadpoles: Generally similar to Common Frog (page 87) but with
brownish-grey coloration and LTRF 4–5/4
IUCN Red List: Least Concern

Left This large brown frog inhabits mountain streams from south-eastern Europe.

Greek Stream Frog – *Rana graeca*

This species is a large version of the Italian Stream Frog (page 91) and has a similar ecology. It differs from the sympatric Common Frog (page 87) and Moor Frog (page 88) in having long hindlimbs, and from the Agile Frog (page 89) by its dark throat. It is unclear whether it has contact with the Italian Agile Frog (page 90), whose nostrils are closer together. Males call from calm waters, but their sounds are usually masked by the river noise and so might not be that important. They are sometimes predated by water snakes and crayfish.

Identification Criteria

① Stocky, flat body, very similar to Italian Stream Frog but larger
② Long hindlimbs (leg test: exceeding the snout)
③ Dark throat with a median line
④ Between-nostrils distance > eye–nostril distance

Size: 7–8cm
Habitat: Fresh mountain streams in forest areas, as well as caves and irrigation channels; up to 2,000m
Reproductive Period: February–April
Sexual Dimorphism: As for Italian Stream Frog
Call: As for Italian Stream Frog
Spawn/Tadpoles: As for Italian Stream Frog
IUCN Red List: Least Concern

Left Coloration is variable, as seen here in this pale brown individual.

Right The dark throat helps to distinguish this species from the Common Frog.

Iberian Frog – *Rana iberica*

A small, slender species, the Iberian Frog often has beautiful marbled coloration. In contrast to other brown frogs, it is not unusual to find this species during the day, close to mountain streams in humid forest areas. It has also been reported breeding in cave-like habitats. Very agile, it will jump quickly to escape when disturbed. The Iberian Frog is threatened by habitat loss, as well as by invasive species of fish and American Mink (*Neovison vison*) that have escaped from fur farms.

Identification Criteria
1. Medium-sized hindlimbs (leg test: reaching or slightly exceeding the snout)
2. Small, discreet tympanum
3. Fully webbed feet (the sympatric *Rana temporaria parvipalmata* from north-west Spain has reduced webbing)
4. Dark throat with white central line (pale throat in Common Frog; page 87)

Size: 4–6cm

Habitat: Humid forests in the north-eastern Iberian mountains; up to 2,400m

Reproductive Period: November–March, until June–July at high altitudes

Sexual Dimorphism: Males have grey nuptial calluses on their thumbs

Call: Guttural, low-pitched, almost toad-like *rao-rao-rao* (3 notes per second)

Spawn: Eggs small (4–7mm with capsule); deposited in small clutches (100–400 eggs) under rocks or among shallow aquatic vegetation

Tadpoles: Generally similar to Common Frog but greyish and with spotted coloration patterns

IUCN Red List: Near Threatened

Left The tadpole of this species is much darker than in other brown frogs.

Right This species is only found in some mountain streams in the Pyrenees.

Pyrenean Frog – *Rana pyrenaica*

Mostly restricted to the Spanish side of the Pyrenees, the Pyrenean Frog is the smallest brown frog in Europe. It is also one of the few European amphibians exclusively associated with mountain habitats. It can be confused only with the Common Frog (page 87), but that species is usually bigger and has a pointier snout, more contrasting markings (spots) and a larger, more visible tympanum. Adults are essentially aquatic, while juveniles spend more time on the ground. Deposited in moving waters, the eggs are heavy and dense to prevent them from floating away. Extremely localised, the species is one of the most endangered amphibians in Europe and locality coordinates are usually kept secret for conservation reasons.

Identification Criteria
1. Rounded snout and well-spaced nostrils (between-nostril distance > between-eyes distance)
2. Small, discreet tympanum
3. Medium-sized hindlimbs (leg test: reaching or slightly exceeding the snout)
4. Fully webbed feet

Size: 3–5cm
Habitat: Mountain streams with cold, fresh, well-oxygenated water; altitudes of 1,000–2,000m
Reproductive Period: February–April, after the snow cover has thawed
Sexual Dimorphism: Males have pale nuptial pads on their thumbs
Call: Low-pitched grunts of low intensity, carrying only a short distance
Spawn: Eggs very large (>1cm), in dense capsule; deposited in small clumps (<150) under stones, in crevices or on the stream bed
Tadpoles: Generally similar to other brown frogs, but coloration very dark (similar to that of the Spiny Toad; page 73) with white pigmentation; low upper tail fin and rounded tail tip; LTRF 4/4
IUCN Red List: Endangered

Left When threatened, this species raises its hands as a reflex.

Right The tadpole of *Rana macrocnemis* is much lighter than other brown frogs.

Long-legged Wood Frog – *Rana macrocnemis*

Also called Caucasus Frog, the Long-legged Wood Frog (whose legs are not actually that long compared to those of some European brown frogs) is the nominal species of the taxonomically controversial Anatolian mountain frogs group, which also includes the Tavas Frog (page 96) and is related to the Hyrcanian Frog (page 97). For a long period, authors also considered local morphotypes described as *R. holtzi* and *R. camerani* to be distinct species, but genetic analyses revealed that these were referrable to *R. macrocnemis* and do not constitute separate entities. When threatened, the Long-legged Wood Frog exhibits a defensive posture similar to the unken reflex of *Bombina* species (page 25).

Identification Criteria
① Medium-sized hindlimbs (leg test: reaching or slightly exceeding the snout)
② Granulated skin
③ Pale dorsal line usually present
④ Often has a prominent white upper lip

Size: 5–8cm
Habitat: Mountain forests and steppes, as well as alpine and subalpine meadows, often close to swamps, lakes, rivers and springs; up to 3,000m
Reproductive Period: March–June
Sexual Dimorphism: Males have nuptial pads on the first finger
Call: Low croaking call *k'oar...k'oar...k'oar*
Spawn: Generally similar to Common Frog (page 87)
Tadpoles: Generally similar to other brown frogs, but coloration lighter (usually brownish) and LTRF usually 3/4
IUCN Red List: Least Concern

Left This species is endemic to two areas in Turkey – notably Elmali near Antalya, and the Tavas region.

Tavas Frog – *Rana tavasensis*

A very localised species, originally known from a single brook, the Tavas Frog is now documented in two areas in south-western Turkey: the Tavas region, from which it gets its name; and the Elmali region further south. Genetic analyses supported its specific status. Additional phylogeographic analyses will be required to understand its exact distribution and allow its precarious conservation situation to be updated. The species is a clear example of the uniqueness of the Lycian region for herpetofauna, where many amphibians – notably the *Lyciasalamandra* group (pages 170–77) – display endemic diversity.

Identification Criteria
Morphologically identical to Long-legged Wood Frog (page 95) and distinguishable only by distribution (see map)

Size: 4–7cm
Habitat: Forests and grasslands, usually with rivers; altitudes around 1,500m
Reproductive Period: March–June
Sexual Dimorphism: As for Long-legged Wood Frog
Call: As for Long-legged Wood Frog
Spawn/Tadpoles: Supposedly similar to Long-legged Wood Frog
IUCN Red List: Endangered

Right With its very long legs and brown coloration, this species cannot be confused with other frogs from the Hyrcanian region.

Hyrcanian Frog – *Rana pseudodalmatina*

This Iranian endemic was formerly considered a subspecies of the Long-legged Wood Frog (page 95), with which it shares many features. It is, however, well differentiated on genetic grounds, and can be separated by a few morphological criteria. Along with some other amphibian species (including Eichwald's Toad, page 75), it is restricted to the southern shore of the Caspian Sea, having survived the dry glacial periods of the Quaternary in the mild conditions of the area.

Identification Criteria
Similar to Long-legged Wood Frog but:
① Slender body and smooth skin
② No pale dorsal band
③ Thin, short white upper lip

Size: 5–8cm
Habitat: Forests and grasslands, usually close to rivers
Reproductive Period: February– April
Sexual Dimorphism: As for Long-legged Wood Frog
Call: Supposedly similar to Long-legged Wood Frog
Spawn/Tadpoles: As for Long-legged Wood Frog
IUCN Red List: Least Concern

Ranidae – Genus *Pelophylax*

Without doubt, the most challenging anurans to identify are the *Pelophylax* water frogs, which are widespread throughout Eurasia and North Africa. The genus contains about 25 species, including 16 in the Western Palearctic. Superficially resembling brown frogs, water frogs spend much of their active time in the water. They tend to favour lowlands and breed in warmer conditions later in the season (April–July). *Pelophylax* are very common: everyone has some in their garden pond or has heard their mocking, laughing calls while walking around wetlands.

The main reason water frogs are hard to separate from one another is the propensity of some sympatric species to hybridise in a peculiar fashion called hybridogenesis. In this process, the two parental genomes are not mixed together during gamete production in the hybrids, because one is eliminated beforehand. As such, the hybrids always have a stable genetic background, with 50 per cent of each parental genome, and are considered species on their own, usually designated as 'kleptons' (abbreviated kl.). Hence, we

can generally distinguish three types of coexisting water frogs: the pool frogs, the marsh frogs and their hybridogenetic hybrids, the edible frogs. Apart from genetics, the sole relatively reliable way to distinguish sympatric species is to inspect the metatarsal tubercle on the first toe.

In the Western Palearctic, pool frogs include the European Pool Frog (*Pelophylax lessonae*; central and western Europe), Italian Pool Frog (*P. bergeri*; Italy and Tyrrhenian islands) and Albanian Water Frog (*P. shqipericus*; Balkans). Two additional species that diverged early on inhabit Iberia (Perez's Frog, *P. perezi*) and North Africa (Sahara Frog, *P. saharicus*). Marsh frogs, nominally represented by the widespread Eurasian Marsh Frog (*P. ridibundus*), are extremely diverse and feature multiple species/species complexes in the Balkans (Balkan Frog, *P. kurtmuelleri*, and Epirus Water Frog, *P. epeiroticus*), Anatolia (Levant Water Frog, *P. bedriagae*, and Beyşehir Water Frog, *P. caralitanus*) and eastern Mediterranean islands (Cretan Frog, *P. cretensis*, Cyprus Water Frog, *P. cypriensis*, and Karpathos Frog, *P. cerigensis*). So far, three hybridogenetic

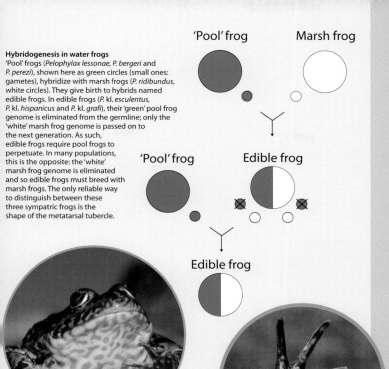

Hybridogenesis in water frogs
'Pool' frogs (*Pelophylax lessonae, P. bergeri* and *P. perezi*), shown here as green circles (small ones: gametes), hybridize with marsh frogs (*P. ridibundus*, white circles). They give birth to hybrids named edible frogs. In edible frogs (*P.* kl. *esculentus, P.* kl. *hispanicus* and *P.* kl. *grafi*), their 'green' pool frog genome is eliminated from the germline; only the 'white' marsh frog genome is passed on to the next generation. As such, edible frogs require pool frogs to perpetuate. In many populations, this is the opposite: the 'white' marsh frog genome is eliminated and so edible frogs must breed with marsh frogs. The only reliable way to distinguish between these three sympatric frogs is the shape of the metatarsal tubercle.

'Pool' frog   Marsh frog

'Pool' frog   Edible frog

Edible frog

Above Some of the species in this family feature unique coloration, as seen here in this Beyşehir Water Frog.

Right Similar to *Rana*, breeding males have large dark nuptial calluses on their first finger.

systems are known, involving the hybrid Edible Frog (*P.* kl. *esculentus* = *P. lessonae* × *P. ridibundus*), Italian Edible Frog (*P.* kl. *hispanicus* = *P. bergeri* × *P. ridibundus*) and Graf's Hybrid Frog (*P.* kl. *grafi* = *P. perezi* × *P. ridibundus*). Given the frequent translocation of frogs throughout Europe, bringing together diverged species that had never met before, along with the cryptic diversity among the marsh frogs, there are probably more hybridogenetic complexes yet to be discovered.

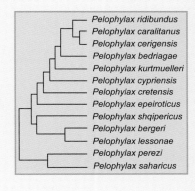

- *Pelophylax ridibundus*
- *Pelophylax caralitanus*
- *Pelophylax cerigensis*
- *Pelophylax bedriagae*
- *Pelophylax kurtmuelleri*
- *Pelophylax cypriensis*
- *Pelophylax cretensis*
- *Pelophylax epeiroticus*
- *Pelophylax shqipericus*
- *Pelophylax bergeri*
- *Pelophylax lessonae*
- *Pelophylax perezi*
- *Pelophylax saharicus*

Left Males fold their lateral vocal sac in slits below the tympanum.

Right The semicircular metatarsal tubercle is characteristic of pool frogs

European Pool Frog – *Pelophylax lessonae*

Size, coloration and, most importantly, the shape of the metatarsal tubercle allow the widespread European Pool Frog to be tentatively separated from its syntopic congener, the Eurasian Marsh Frog (page 105), and their hybridogenetic hybrid, the Edible Frog (page 113). Originally, only European Pool and Edible frogs colonised western Europe, but the introduction of Eurasian Marsh Frogs is now disrupting the equilibrium of this hybridogenetic complex. As such, the European Pool Frog is highly threatened in this region, but its conservation and management are challenging due to the difficulties of field identification. In western Europe, populations have also been cryptically replaced by the Italian Pool Frog (page 101).

Identification Criteria
1. Medium-sized frog with a horizontal pupil and green coloration, usually including patches and a dorsal line
2. No temporal spot
3. Large semicircular metatarsal tubercle and short first toe
4. Yellow or brown groin and inner thighs
5. White vocal sacs
6. Short legs (leg test: not reaching the eyes)

Size: 4–7cm
Habitat: Small, sunny water bodies with rich vegetation; up to 1,500m
Reproductive Period: May–July
Sexual Dimorphism: Females are larger than males; males have a pair of lateral vocal sacs under the tympanum (internally folded when at rest) and grey nuptial pads on the first finger
Call: Squeaking series of guttural croaks, rrrraoow… rrrraoow… rrrraoow (each note lasting 1.5 seconds), emitted day and night
Spawn: Eggs small (6–8mm with capsule); clutches (up to 3,000 eggs) deposited in multiple small grapes on aquatic vegetation close to the surface
Tadpoles: Medium-sized tadpole, 4–8cm; brown or olive coloration, becoming green with age; spiracle sinistral, diagonally oriented upward; cloaca dextral; tail tip pointy; LTRF 2–3/3
IUCN Red List: Least Concern

Left Pool frogs lay eggs in grapes of several hundred.

Right Tadpoles are an olive colour and can already show dark spots.

Italian Pool Frog – *Pelophylax bergeri*

This is the sister species of the European Pool Frog (page 100), and it is found in Italy south of the Apennines, and in Corsica and Sardinia. Populations from Sicily might belong to another distinct taxon. The species also appears to inhabit a large portion of western Europe, including Switzerland, France and Germany, but was confused with the European Pool Frog (with which it hybridised hugely) before the era of modern genetics. As the analysis of museum specimens suggests, its presence there might predate modern times and originate from old translocations that took place during antiquity. In its natural Italian range, the Italian Pool Frog is usually sympatric with its hybridogenetic hybrid, the Italian Edible Frog (page 114).

Identification Criteria
Morphologically identical to European Pool Frog and distinguishable only by distribution (see map)

Size: 5–8cm
Habitat: As for European Pool Frog; up to 1,800m
Reproductive Period: March–June
Sexual Dimorphism: As for European Pool Frog
Call: As for European Pool Frog
Spawn/Tadpoles: As for European Pool Frog
IUCN Red List: Least Concern

Left Coloration is highly variable, spanning from grey/brown to fully green.

Albanian Water Frog – *Pelophylax shqipericus*

The very localised Albanian Water Frog inhabits 60km of the Adriatic shoreline in Albania and southern Montenegro, where it is also found in Lake Skadar. It lives in highly vegetated water bodies and is threatened due to its narrow range. Its evolution echoes the past isolation of populations within the Balkans, which drove the divergence of multiple amphibian species. The Albanian Water Frog can be found together with the Balkan Frog (page 106), but differs in its coloration and the shape of its metatarsal tubercle. These two species may hybridise in a classic manner (in other words, not by hybridogenesis), whereby the parental genomes are mixed up generation after generation.

Identification Criteria
Similar to European Pool Frog (page 100) but:
① Larger on average
② Olive-grey vocal sacs

Size: 5–8cm
Habitat: Freshwater marshes, swamps and ditches, as well as lake shorelines; up to 500m
Reproductive Period: March–August
Sexual Dimorphism: Similar to European Pool Frog, but vocal sacs of males are olive-grey
Call: As for European Pool Frog
Spawn/Tadpoles: As for European Pool Frog
IUCN Red List: Endangered

Left In water frogs, vocal sacs are lateral; their colour can help with identification.

Right Perez's Frogs have small, flat metatarsal tubercles.

Perez's Frog – *Pelophylax perezi*

A native of Iberia, this common species was introduced to Madeira, as well as the Canary and Balearic islands. Quite different in appearance to pool frogs, Perez's Frog is more like a small version of the Eurasian Marsh Frog (page 105). The two were once considered conspecific, but fortunately for identification purposes they do not naturally co-occur. In Catalonia and southern France, however, Perez's Frog is found together with its hybridogenetic klepton, Graf's Hybrid Frog (page 115), although it is much smaller and has flat metatarsal tubercles (oval in Graf's). Illegal introductions of *Pelophylax kurtmuelleri, P. bedriagae* and *P. ridibundus* in southern France might threaten Perez's Frog in the future.

Identification Criteria
Similar to Eurasian Marsh Frog, but smaller, and sharing the following features:
(1) Tiny, flat metatarsal tubercles
(2) Green, grey or brown coloration
(3) Inner thighs and groin greyish or white (not yellow as in pool frogs)

Size: 5–9cm
Habitat: All kinds of water bodies; up to 2,300m
Reproductive Period: February–June
Sexual Dimorphism: Females are larger than males; males have grey vocal sacs and nuptial pads on the fingers
Call: Grunting, resonant *rehehehehe… rehehehehe* (each lasting ~1.5 seconds), similar to the call of the Edible Frog (page 113)
Spawn: As for European Pool Frog (page 100); total clutch size up to 10,000 eggs
Tadpoles: Similar to European Pool Frog except LTRF is generally 1/3
IUCN Red List: Least Concern

Left Sahara Frogs can be found in all kinds of freshwater habitats. Their coloration spans from brown to green, with many patches.

Sahara Frog – *Pelophylax saharicus*

This large species is the only water frog present in North Africa, and its identification is therefore straightforward. Ecologically versatile, the Sahara Frog inhabits a wide range of habitats, from alpine areas to semi-deserts along the northern edge of the Sahara. In comparison to some other species adapted to arid environments, it does not aestivate but remains active even during the driest months of the summer. Genetic studies are unravelling a cryptic diversity among this widespread species, which may see its taxonomy revised in the near future.

Identification Criteria
Morphologically identical to Perez's Frog (page 103) and Eurasian Marsh Frog (page 105), and distinguishable only by distribution (see map)

Size: 5–10cm
Habitat: All types of freshwater habitats, including streams, ponds, lakes and irrigation canals, in meadows, bushland and oases; up to 2,600m
Reproductive Period: Usually March–May
Sexual Dimorphism: As for Perez's Frog
Call: As for Perez's Frog
Spawn: As for European Pool Frog (page 100); total clutch size up to 10,000 eggs
Tadpoles: As for European Pool Frog
Subspecies: Two (page 198)
IUCN Red List: Least Concern

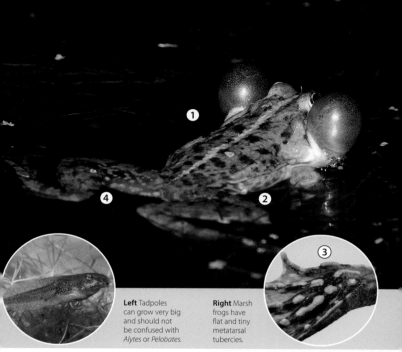

Left Tadpoles can grow very big and should not be confused with *Alytes* or *Pelobates*.

Right Marsh frogs have flat and tiny metatarsal tubercles.

Eurasian Marsh Frog – *Pelophylax ridibundus*

Widespread, ubiquitous, loud and abundant, the Eurasian Marsh Frog is the amphibian species many people have both seen and heard. One of the biggest anurans of the continent, the species was imported to western Europe as part of the trade in frogs' legs. Escaping from farms as early as the 1950s, the frogs subsequently colonised most of Belgium, France, Germany and Switzerland, and currently threaten many species through competition and hybridisation. This voracious species also preys on smaller amphibians. The extremely high diversity displayed among populations in Anatolia and the Middle East should lead to the description of new species in the years to come.

Identification Criteria
1. Very large with green, greyish or brownish coloration
2. Inner thighs and groin greyish or white (not yellow)
3. Small, flat metatarsal tubercles
4. Medium-sized legs (leg test: reaching the eye)

Size: Up to 15cm
Habitat: Almost all lowland habitats, including forests, steppes and deserts, with flowing or stagnant waters, and usually with well-exposed, rich herbaceous vegetation; tolerates estuary salinity
Reproductive Period: March–July
Sexual Dimorphism: Females are larger than males; males have grey or dark nuptial pads on the fingers and grey vocal sacs
Call: Has a rich repertoire of complex, varied calls that are difficult to transcribe, the most common being a loud *kekekekekekekek* series of ascending and descending tones (lasting 1 second), reminiscent of a laugh, and individual *rrrooooak* croaks; can be heard from a long distance day and night
Spawn: As for European Pool Frog (page 100); total clutch size <15,000 eggs
Tadpoles: Similar to European Pool Frog, but can grow enormous (>15cm)
IUCN Red List: Least Concern

Left Some individuals, notably juveniles, are brownish.

Right The metatarsal tubercle resembles that of the Marsh Frog.

Balkan Frog – *Pelophylax kurtmuelleri*

This cousin of the Eurasian Marsh Frog (page 105) was described in the early 1990s based on bioacoustic analyses. It also differs genetically from that species, but the long history of hybridisation between the two complicates their taxonomic position. The two species are morphologically similar. On the western edges of its natural distribution, the Balkan Frog meets and can admix with the Albanian Water Frog (page 102) and Epirus Water Frogs (page 107). The species has also been introduced in several places across western Europe, including Denmark, Switzerland, Italy and France. In the latter, it might even have started a new hybridogenetic complex with Perez's Frog (page 103), which is pending further investigations.

Identification Criteria

1. Small, flat metatarsal tubercle (shape differs in Albanian and Epirus water frogs)
2. Prominent dorsal folds (discreet in Epirus Water Frog)
3. Inner thighs and groin greyish or white (yellowish in Albanian and Epirus Water Frogs)

Size: 6–10cm
Habitat: All freshwater habitats, but favours open, sunny waters; up to 1,000m
Reproductive Period: March–July
Sexual Dimorphism: As for Eurasian Marsh Frog
Call: Generally similar to Eurasian Marsh Frog but individual calls are shorter (0.5 seconds)
Spawn/Tadpoles: As for European Pool Frog (page 100)
IUCN Red List: Least Concern

Right Other than the shape of the metatarsal tubercle, this species differs from other sympatric species by its yellowish groin.

Epirus Water Frog – *Pelophylax epeiroticus*

A threatened species endemic to western Greece, including the island of Corfu, as well as south-western Albania, the Epirus Water Frog can be found together, and frequently hybridises, with the Balkan Frog (page 106). Hybrids, however, remain in low proportions among mixed populations. Some behaviours of the Epirus Water Frog are peculiar: it calls while hidden under floating vegetation, with only its head emerging (in contrast, other marsh frogs usually float at the surface); moreover, it will choose to escape onto land rather than into water (as most water frogs do). Reasons for the species' decline include habitat destruction and pollution, as well as overharvesting for consumption.

Identification Criteria

① Very small, triangle-shaped metatarsal tubercle (longer and flat in Balkan Frog)
② Groin yellowish (grey or white in Balkan Frog)
③ Dorsal folds less prominent than in Balkan Frog

Size: 6–10cm
Habitat: Lowland freshwater habitats with shore vegetation, including large marshes and banks beside calm rivers and canals; up to 500m
Reproductive Period: March–July
Sexual Dimorphism: Similar to Eurasian Marsh Frog (page 105), but vocal sacs are usually olive in colour outside the breeding period
Call: Loud metallic, rattling rrrrrrreh… rrrrrrreh… rrrrrrreh (0.5 seconds per note); hybrids with the Balkan Frog make calls like the European Pool Frog (page 100)
Spawn/Tadpoles: As for European Pool Frog
IUCN Red List: Vulnerable

Left This Cretan endemic inhabits marshes in the lowlands, close to the shores of the island.

Cretan Frog – *Pelophylax cretensis*

As both its common and scientific names suggest, this species is endemic to Crete, where it inhabits coastal marshes, lakes and streams. It is rarely abundant, the loss of aquatic habitat due to water extraction for industrial agriculture (notably banana plantations), combined with urbanisation linked to tourism development, being a major concern for the highly fragmented populations. The invasive American Bullfrog (page 116) might also outcompete the Cretan Frog in some parts of the island.

Identification Criteria
Similar to Eurasian Marsh Frog (page 105) but:
① Usually brown-grey coloration, sometimes greenish with brown spots
② Groin and inner thighs yellowish
③ Metatarsal tubercle more developed than in continental marsh frogs

Size: 5–8cm
Habitat: Coastal wetlands and slow-moving streams
Reproductive Period: March–June
Sexual Dimorphism: As for Eurasian Marsh Frog
Call: Fast, metallic *rehihihihihihihihihi*, similar to (but higher in pitch than) the calls of Perez's Frog (page 103) and the Edible Frog (page 113)
Spawn/Tadpoles: As for European Pool Frog (page 100)
IUCN Red List: Endangered

Left Levant specimens are genetically unique, despite similar coloration to other populations.

Right Note the resemblance to *P. ridibundus*, with which its range overlaps.

Levant Water Frog – *Pelophylax bedriagae*

Confusingly, this is not an individual species but a species complex: originally described from the Levant region, it includes multiple lineages throughout Anatolia that may deserve specific status pending further studies and description. In addition, the similar-looking Eurasian Marsh Frog (page 105) also occurs in the region and hybridises with the Levant Water Frog. The status of many populations is thus unclear, since in the field the two differ only in their subtly dissimilar mating calls. In fact, many water frogs introduced to western Europe are a mixture between the two species. The Levant Water Frog was given its species name in honour of the Russian herpetologist Jacques von Bedriaga (1854–1906).

Identification Criteria
Morphologically identical to Eurasian Marsh Frog and distinguishable only by distribution (see map)

Size: 6–10cm
Habitat: All types of swampy habitats with vegetation, including wetlands, ponds, streams, canals and marshes
Reproductive Period: February–July
Sexual Dimorphism: As for Eurasian Marsh Frog
Call: As for Cretan Frog (page 108)
Spawn/Tadpoles: As for European Pool Frog (page 100)
IUCN Red List: Least Concern

Left This is the type specimen that was used for the description of this species.

Right Juveniles are often a duller colour and appear rounded.

Cyprus Water Frog – *Pelophylax cypriensis*

The Cyprus Water Frog is endemic to the island that gave it its name. Like many other Mediterranean taxa, it is a remnant of old geological processes. About six million years ago, the Mediterranean Basin was closed off and the sea progressively dried out, thereby linking many continental and island populations across land bridges. This epoch, known as the Messinian salinity crisis, ended 5.3 million years ago, when the Strait of Gibraltar opened and the Mediterranean Sea refilled. The event initiated island–continent evolutionary divergence that ultimately led to the creation of distinct species, as here with the Cyprus Water Frog. Morphologically, this taxon is similar to the mainland species (pages 105 and 109).

Identification Criteria
Similar to Eurasian Marsh Frog (page 105) but:
① Generally brown, greyish, olive or light green in colour

Size: 6–10cm
Habitat: Wide spectrum of habitats, including wetlands, streams, pools and ditches; up to 1,400m
Reproductive Period: March–June
Sexual Dimorphism: As for Eurasian Marsh Frog
Call: Generally similar to Levant Water Frog (page 109) but calls are shorter with fewer notes: *rehihihihihi*
Spawn/Tadpoles: As for European Pool Frog (page 100)
IUCN Red List: —

Left The dorsal line is present in many *Pelophylax* species, including this one.

Right Instead of a line, some individuals feature spots on the dorsum.

Beyşehir Water Frog – *Pelophylax caralitanus*

A close relative of the Levant Water Frog (page 109), this species is endemic to the Turkish Lake District in south-western Anatolia. It was originally described as a Turkish subspecies of the Eurasian Marsh Frog (page 105), and latterly of the Levant Water Frog in the late 1980s, based on the distinctive orange coloration of its belly. Herpetologists used this criterion to delimit its geographic range. Later, genetic studies confirmed the uniqueness of the taxon, but additional analyses will be necessary to understand the extent to which it hybridises with the Levant Water Frog.

Identification Criteria
Similar to Eurasian Marsh Frog (page 105) but:
① Ventral side has orange maculation

Size: 5–10cm
Habitat: Permanent wetlands with rich vegetation, ponds, streams, channels and marshes on lake shorelines
Reproductive Period: March–June
Sexual Dimorphism: As for Eurasian Marsh Frog
Call: As for to Levant Water Frog
Spawn/Tadpoles: As for European Pool Frog (page 100)
IUCN Red List: Near Threatened

Left This tiny individual is nevertheless a reproducing adult; the Karpathos Frog is a dwarf species which is a common feature on islands.

Karpathos Frog – *Pelophylax cerigensis*

The most localised *Pelophylax* species, the Karpathos Frog is consequently also the most threatened by extinction. So far confirmed only from the Aegean island of Karpathos, which lies between Crete and Turkey, it is known from a single river on the north side of the island (near the town of Olympos). Karpathos has been isolated for at least three million years, but genetic data indicate that at some stage the gene pool of the Karpathos Frog reached neighbouring Rhodes and the Anatolian mainland. The exact nature of these populations is pending analyses. Smaller than other water frogs, the Karpathos Frog is the only *Pelophylax* species to inhabit its namesake island and thus cannot be confused.

Identification Criteria
Similar to Eurasian Marsh Frog (page 105) but:
① Small, with brown or olive coloration

Size: 4–6cm
Habitat: Still and slow-running river waters from northern Karpathos
Reproductive Period: March–June
Sexual Dimorphism: As for Eurasian Marsh Frog
Call: Generally similar to Levant Water Frog (page 109), but calls are shorter with fewer notes, *rehihihihihi*, like those of the Cyprus Water Frog (page 110)
Spawn/Tadpoles: Presumably similar to European Pool Frog (page 100)
IUCN Red List: Critically Endangered

Left The tubercle is intermediate to that of its parental species *P. lessonae* and *P. ridibundus*.

Right Edible Frogs are voracious and can prey on other amphibians.

Edible Frog – *Pelophylax* kl. *esculentus*

The Edible Frog arose from hybridogenetic crosses between the European Pool Frog (*Pelophylax lessonae*; page 100) and Eurasian Marsh Frog (*P. ridibundus*; page 105), and hence features many intermediate morphological characters. In western Europe, *P.* kl. *esculentus* contributes gametes (eggs and sperm) only with its *ridibundus* genome, and so it must breed with *P. lessonae* in order to perpetuate. In eastern ranges, the opposite is generally the case. Some populations are all hybrids (in other words, composed only of *P.* kl. *esculentus*) and survive because one parental genome is duplicated, resulting in triploid individuals (*lessonae/ lessonae/ridibundus* and *lessonae/ ridibundus/ridibundus*).

Identification Criteria

Generally similar in appearance and coloration to European Pool Frog but:

① Body and leg size intermediate between European Pool Frog and Eurasian Marsh Frog
② Medium-sized metatarsal tubercle, often asymmetric (larger and semicircular in European Pool Frog, small and flat in Eurasian Marsh Frog)

Size: 7–12cm
Habitat: As for the parental species, including all types of sunny wetlands, ponds and canals with vegetation
Reproductive Period: May–July
Sexual Dimorphism: Females are larger than males; males have white, grey or black vocal sacs and grey or black nuptial pads, and bright green or yellow tints in the breeding season (as in European Pool Frog)
Call: Grunting, resonant *rehehehehe* (~1.5 seconds per note)
Spawn/Tadpoles: Similar to European Pool Frog; total clutch <10,000 eggs
IUCN Red List: —

Left This species generally resembles its syntopic parent *P. bergeri*.

Right The tubercle of this hybrid is intermediate between that of its parental species.

Italian Edible Frog – *Pelophylax* kl. *hispanicus*

The hybridogenetic hybrid between the Eurasian Marsh Frog (*Pelophylax ridibundus*; page 105) and Italian Pool Frog (*P. bergeri*; page 101), the Italian Edible Frog coexists and breeds with the latter throughout most of the Apennine Peninsula and Sicily. Its origin is puzzling, because the Eurasian Marsh Frog has never been observed in Italy. Even more puzzling is the fact that the hybrid's *ridibundus* genome shares ancestry with Anatolian populations; how and when hybridogenesis was initiated in the first place thus remains an open question. As in other water frog systems, discriminating Italian Edible Frogs from Italian Pool Frogs requires inspection of their metatarsal tubercles.

Identification Criteria

Generally similar in appearance to Italian Pool Frog but:
1. Medium-sized metatarsal tubercle, often asymmetric (larger and semicircular in Italian Pool Frog)
2. Groin and inner thighs rarely yellow but with white spots (yellow in Italian Pool Frog)
3. Vocal sacs dark grey (white in Italian Pool Frog)

Size: Up to 10cm
Habitat: Shares the same habitats as Italian Pool Frog
Reproductive Period: Simultaneous with Italian Pool Frog
Sexual Dimorphism: Females are larger than males; males have dark grey vocal sacs and nuptial pads
Call: As for Edible Frog (page 113)
Spawn/Tadpoles: As for European Pool Frog (page 100)
IUCN Red List: —

Right Intriguingly, the tubercle of *P.* kl *grafi* is not the intermediate between its parental species, where it is small and flat for both.

Graf's Hybrid Frog – *Pelophylax* kl. *grafi*

Graf's Hybrid Frog is a klepton found together with Perez's Frog (*Pelophylax perezi*; page 103) in Catalonia and southern France, on which it relies for reproduction. As in the other hybridogenetic systems in the genus, the second parental species is the Eurasian Marsh Frog (*P. ridibundus*; page 105), or rather its ancestor since the species is not naturally present in the area. However, Eurasian Marsh Frogs now occur in several places in the region following the release of imports, and may compromise the *perezi–grafi* equilibrium. Graf's Hybrid Frog can be distinguished from its parental species thanks to the shape of its metatarsal tubercle.

Identification Criteria
Generally similar in appearance and coloration to Perez's and Eurasian Marsh Frogs but:
① Larger than Perez's Frog
② Medium-sized metatarsal tubercle (small and flat in Perez's Frog and Eurasian Marsh Frog)

Size: 5–11cm
Habitat: Shares the same habitats as Perez's Frog
Reproductive Period: Simultaneous with Perez's Frog
Sexual Dimorphism: As for Eurasian Marsh Frog
Call: Similar to Eurasian Marsh Frog, but with longer pauses between notes
Spawn/Tadpoles: Supposedly similar to European Pool Frog (page 100)
IUCN Red List: —

Left Do not confuse these tadpoles with large *Pelophylax* ones.

Right Metamorphs are already bigger than some other adult anurans at metamorphosis.

EXOTIC SPECIES American Bullfrog – *Lithobates catesbeianus*

Originating in the eastern part of North America, the American Bullfrog is one of the biggest anurans on Earth. In Europe, it was originally introduced to the Po Plain in Italy, but is now found in many adjacent countries. Reasons for its import were multiple: for the pet trade, as a biological control agent against ravaging insects, and for harvesting for food and its skin (used for leather goods). The invasion in south-western France stems from releases by a French aviator in the late 1960s, who brought back some specimens for his backyard pond. The species is a successful invader due to the lack of natural predators and its strong competitive and dispersal capabilities. Eradication plans are ongoing.

Identification Criteria
① Huge green frog with an enormous tympanum
② No dorsal fold as in European water frogs
③ Vocal sac on the throat (not on the side as in European water frogs)

Size: Up to 20cm
Habitat: Lake and river shores, and ponds in meadows and pastures, usually with abundant vegetation; up to 400m
Reproductive Period: April–August
Sexual Dimorphism: Males have a yellowish throat and vocal sac, and a much bigger tympanum (twice the eye diameter) than females
Call: Very strong, mooing *broaam… broaam… broaam*, like the roaring of a bull, hence its name
Spawn: Eggs 8–10mm with capsule; laid in a flattened floating mass (10,000–20,000 eggs)
Tadpoles: Large (up to 16cm), with the same general characteristics as *Pelophylax*: spiracle sinistral, diagonally oriented upward; cloaca dextral; tail tip pointy; dorsal side is olive in colour with wrinkles; ventral side is whitish; LTRF 3/4
IUCN Red List: Least Concern

Left The tadpoles of this species are reminiscent of a catfish.

Right This scavenging species has claws on its hind feet, used to tear food apart.

African Clawed Frog – *Xenopus laevis*

Literally meaning 'smooth, strange foot', the name *Xenopus laevis* comes from the species' soft skin and the claws on its hind feet. The African Clawed Frog is a popular pet and has been a research subject since the 1930s, used for pregnancy tests in the 1950s, for pioneer studies in various fields like developmental, cell and neural biology, and even for space research – it flew aboard the Space Shuttle *Endeavour* in 1992! Naturally distributed from sub-Saharan Africa to South Africa, it is a pest in several European countries. In all areas where it is non-native, it is invasive and threatens local amphibians by eating their eggs and larvae, and by being an asymptomatic vector of chytridomycosis and ranaviruses.

Identification Criteria
1. Flat, smooth body
2. Small eyes on the top of the head
3. Fully webbed hind feet
4. Completely aquatic; usually found in water

Size: 5–14cm
Habitat: In Europe, usually favours disturbed or man-made permanent water bodies such as drainage ditches and irrigation canals, but can be found in many types of ponds
Reproductive Period: March–July
Sexual Dimorphism: Females are larger than males and, when gravid, have hip-like bulges at the base of the abdomen
Call: Metallic, rattling rrrrreeee-rrrrreeee-rrrrreeee
Spawn: Single eggs or small grape-like clusters are laid on aquatic plants or rocks; >10,000 eggs per clutch
Tadpoles: Slender shape with barbels, making it reminiscent of a catfish; cannot be confused with other anuran tadpoles
IUCN Red List: Least Concern

CAUDATA

Salamandridae 1 – Small Newts

Salamandridae is a large family of newts and true salamanders from the northern hemisphere. About 80 species are known, many of them present across the Western Palearctic. Reproductive strategies vary significantly between and even among species. All newts and some salamanders are oviparous: they lay eggs in the water, which hatch into larvae that later metamorphose into juveniles. Salamanders can be larviparous (giving birth to larvae) and/or viviparous (giving birth to fully formed juveniles). The rich Salamandridae diversity is treated here across six separate sections.

Small newts mate in a peculiar way, with the male flicking his tail to seduce the female. In this courtship ritual, the male performs three kinds of movements in a static display: the fan, a delicate vibration with the tail flexed along his body; the whip, a vigorous lash of the tail against his flank; and the wave, where the tail is held more or less perpendicular to the flank and is slowly undulated. During this show, the male also emits pheromones that spread thanks to the water currents created by his tail movements. If the female is receptive, the male then releases a spermatophore (a bag full of his sperm), which she vacuums into her cloaca to fertilise her eggs internally. Eggs are carefully attached to aquatic vegetation and hatch into carnivorous larvae, which prey on small aquatic animals. Some larvae reach sexual maturity before metamorphosis; these are termed neotenic or paedomorphic, and retain larval traits (e.g. gills) throughout their entire life. Small newts are crepuscular, being seen mostly at night and hiding in aquatic vegetation during the day.

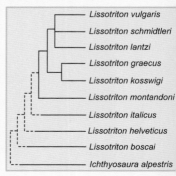

Lissotriton vulgaris
Lissotriton schmidtleri
Lissotriton lantzi
Lissotriton graecus
Lissotriton kosswigi
Lissotriton montandoni
Lissotriton italicus
Lissotriton helveticus
Lissotriton boscai
Ichthyosaura alpestris

Left Males displays more flashy colours than females, especially in the Alpine Newt.

Below Outside the breeding season, newts enter a terrestrial phase where they inhabit dry land. They also lose their crests, as seen here in this Smooth Newt.

Left In newts, breeding takes place in the water. Some species, such as this male Palmate Newt, will develop a crest and fringing on the hind feet during this time.

Above, right and far right The sperm is emitted by the male in the form of a bag – the spermatophore – that the female then absorbs with her cloaca (above). Usually, eggs are deposited individually (right). Some individuals retain gills even at the adult stage, in a process called paeodomorphism (far right).

Left Smooth Newts differ from Palmate Newts by their spotted throat.

Right This species has three creases on the head.

Smooth Newt – *Lissotriton vulgaris*

This is the nominal taxon of the *Lissotriton vulgaris* species complex, which includes nine lineages of specific or subspecific status that are widespread throughout Europe and Asia Minor. Smooth Newts are small lowland amphibians, inhabiting a wide range of humid habitats. Two morphotypes of nuptial males exist: one with a linear crest and 'flappy', highly fringed hind feet (*L. v. meridionalis* south of the Alps and *L. v. ampelensis* in Romania); and the other with a ragged, denticulate crest and limited fringing on the hind feet (*L. v. vulgaris*). These morphotypes evolved independently in other species of the complex.

Identification Criteria
(1) Spotted body with crest in males
(2) Dark/greyish spots on belly and throat
(3) Background throat colour lighter than background belly colour
(4) Brownish in terrestrial phase
(5) Three creases on the head
(6) Tail filament absent in males

Size: 6–11cm
Habitat: Various wetlands, ponds, ditches and usually in shallow, sunny situations and with dense vegetation; up to 2,200m
Reproductive Period: March–July
Sexual Dimorphism: Nuptial males have a dorsal crest; bright coloration; a large, bulging cloaca; and some dark fringing on the hind toes/feet
Spawn: 200–300 brownish-white eggs in oval capsules; individually deposited and folded in leaves of aquatic plants
Larvae: Up to 4cm; five hind toes; large, feathery gills; upper and lower tail fins non-parallel; upper tail fin reaching back of head; tail ends progressively, without sting; inter-nostril distance < eye–nostril distance
Subspecies: Three (page 199)
IUCN Red List: —

Left Sexual dimorphism is heavily marked in newts. Here the 'smooth crest' morphotype has a linear crest, developed fringing on hind feet and tail filament in males.

Greek Smooth Newt – *Lissotriton graecus*

Formerly considered a subspecies of the Smooth Newt (page 122), the Greek Smooth Newt merits consideration as a species on its own, as it is restricted to the southern parts of the Balkans (Greece, Albania, Macedonia and Montenegro), is genetically unique and face only limited hybridisation with its former conspecific. Morphologically, the Greek Smooth Newt is smaller than other *Lissotriton* species and usually has a large number of dark spots on its belly. The species falls within the 'smooth crest' morphotype (see page 122), and can thus be recognised from the neighbouring nominate Smooth Newt and Turkish Smooth Newt (page 125), which are of the 'ragged crest' morphotype.

Identification Criteria

Generally similar to Smooth Newt but:
① Linear crest in males, with a weak dorsal ridge present
② Strong fringing on the hind feet in males
③ Tail ends in a long filament in males

Size: 6–9cm
Habitat: Large range of humid habitats, as for Smooth Newt
Reproductive Period: January–May
Sexual Dimorphism: Nuptial males have a linear dorsal crest; tail filament; bright coloration; a large, bulging cloaca; and well-developed dark fringing on the hind feet
Spawn/Larvae: As for Smooth Newt
IUCN Red List: —

Left Unlike males, females have less contrasted markings and lack feet fringing.

Right In this species, the crest begins at the level of the forelimbs.

Kosswig's Smooth Newt – *Lissotriton kosswigi*

Restricted to the south-western shoreline of the Black Sea in Turkey, this newt also bears the hallmark of independent evolutionary history, warranting a specific status. Like its close relative the Greek Smooth Newt (page 123), it is of the 'smooth crest' morphotype. However, Kosswig's Smooth Newt differs in that its crest starts posteriorly, at the level of the forelimbs, not right from the back of the head as in other species. It was named after German zoologist Curt Kosswig (1903–82), who is considered a pioneer of Turkish zoology. This species is most likely threatened due to its narrow distribution.

Identification Criteria
Generally similar to Smooth Newt (page 122) but:
① Crest linear and starts posteriorly, i.e. at the same level of the forelimbs, not the head
② Dorsal ridges well developed
③ Well-developed fringing on the hind feet in males
④ Tail ends in a long filament

Size: 6–8cm
Habitat: Large spectrum of humid habitats, as for Smooth Newt
Reproductive Period: February–May
Sexual Dimorphism: Nuptial males have a linear dorsal crest; tail filament; bright coloration; a large, bulging cloaca; and well-developed dark fringing on the hind feet
Spawn/Larvae: As for Smooth Newt
IUCN Red List: —

Right This species can be easily distinguished from its neighbours as males feature a ragged crest and lack feet fringing and a tail filament.

Turkish Smooth Newt – *Lissotriton schmidtleri*

Distributed in western Anatolia and adjacent areas of south-eastern Europe, this so-called 'dwarf' species is of the 'ragged crest' morphotype, with very pointy spines. It can thus be easily differentiated from its neighbours, Kosswig's Smooth Newt (page 124) in Turkey and the Greek Smooth Newt (page 123) in the Balkans, which are 'smooth crest' newts. However, hybrids at the margin between the species' ranges yield intermediate characters.

Identification Criteria
Generally similar to Smooth Newt (page 122) but:
① Ragged crest with pointy spines
② Very limited fringing on hind toes
③ Tail filament absent

Size: 6–8cm
Habitat: Large range of humid habitats, as for Smooth Newt
Reproductive Period: January–May
Sexual Dimorphism: Nuptial males have a ragged dorsal crest; bright coloration; a large, bulging cloaca; and limited fringing on the hind toes
Spawn/Larvae: As for Smooth Newt
IUCN Red List: —

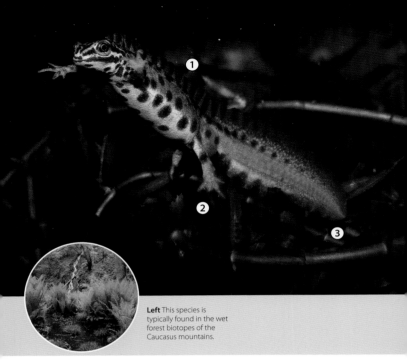

Left This species is typically found in the wet forest biotopes of the Caucasus mountains.

Caucasian Smooth Newt – *Lissotriton lantzi*

Endemic to the Caucasus, this species is found mainly in ponds and wetlands close to forests. Many of its populations are threatened, but like other smooth newt species, it has not received a specific IUCN Red List evaluation since it is often considered part of the *Lissotriton vulgaris* species complex (page 122). The Caucasian Smooth Newt, also commonly known as Lantz's Newt, was given its species name in honour of French herpetologist Louis Lantz (1886–1953), who brought specimens back to France from Russia and Georgia in the early twentieth century.

Identification Criteria

Generally similar to Smooth Newt (page 122) but:
① Ragged crest
② Hind feet fringing moderately well developed
③ Tail ends in a long, fine thread but it lacks a true filament

Size: 6–10cm
Habitat: Ponds, ditches and wetlands, usually in forest areas
Reproductive Period: March–May
Sexual Dimorphism: Nuptial males have a ragged dorsal crest; bright coloration; a large, bulging cloaca; and some fringing on the hind feet
Spawn/Larvae: As for Smooth Newt
IUCN Red List: —

Left This mountainous species inhabits the Carpathians and Tatra ranges.

Right The courtship behaviour in this species is similar to Smooth Newts.

Carpathian Newt – *Lissotriton montandoni*

Closely related to smooth newts, with which it hybridises at the margin of its range, Carpathian Newts are quite different visually. Individuals are greenish with a fully orange belly; females may be confused with female Alpine Newts (page 131), but these have no crease on the head. Males lack a crest and instead have strong dorsal ridges, supposedly evolved to increase the efficiency of fanning movements during courtship. Although the Carpathian Newt is not endangered, it is threatened by landscape changes, especially since alternative breeding sites (e.g. wheel ruts) are usually of poor quality.

Identification Criteria

1. Marbled green or olive back and uniform orange belly
2. Three creases on the head
3. No crest but strongly developed dorsal ridges in males
4. Tail ends in a filament in males

Size: 6–11cm

Habitat: Freshwater marshes, ponds and slow streams, often in or close to coniferous and mixed woodlands and upland pastures; up to 2,000m

Reproductive Period: April–July

Sexual Dimorphism: Males are slightly smaller than females; males have strong dorsal ridges and a filament on the tail

Spawn: As for Smooth Newt (page 122); clutches of 50–250 eggs

Larvae: Similar to Smooth Newt but tail is thin with parallel edges, and ends abruptly in a spike or short filament

IUCN Red List: Least Concern

Left The throat and groin colour can distinguish this species from other small newts.

Right With five toes and feathery gills, the larvae are generally similar to other small newts.

Palmate Newt – *Lissotriton helveticus*

A small newt inhabiting western Europe, from northern Iberia to Germany and the Czech Republic, as well as most of Britain. It can be confused (especially females) with the sympatric nominate Smooth Newt (page 122). The Palmate Newt is the most frequently seen Caudata in many regions of France. Originally described in Switzerland (hence the species epithet *helveticus*), it owes its vernacular name to its highly webbed hind feet. In the winter, the Palmate Newt hibernates under logs or stones.

Identification Criteria
1. Three creases on the head
2. Two tiny white dots present under hind feet
3. Light-coloured patch at insertion of hindlimbs
4. Well-developed dorsal ridges with cryptic dorsal crest in males, well developed on the tail, ending in a dark filament
5. Dark fringing on the hind feet
6. Almost spotless, dull belly and immaculate throat

Size: 6–9cm

Habitat: Various habitats with shallow water bodies, including ponds, ditches and streams, especially in deciduous forests; up to 2,400m

Reproductive Period: March–July

Sexual Dimorphism: Males are slightly smaller than females; males have fringed hind feet, a short filament on the tail and a large, bulging cloaca

Spawn: As for Smooth Newt; clutches of 300–500 eggs

Larvae: As for Smooth Newt but inter-nostril distance = eye–nostril distance

IUCN Red List: Least Concern

Left Similar to other small newts, some individuals can be paedomorphic.

Right The brightly coloured belly is characteristic of Bosca's Newt in the region.

Bosca's Newt – *Lissotriton boscai*

A very special species, Bosca's Newt inhabits the western side of the Iberian Peninsula. In the north of its range, it should not be mistaken for the Palmate Newt (page 128) and Alpine Newt (page 131). Bosca's Newt features a particular courtship element called the 'flamenco', in which the male's static display often ends in him holding his tail vertically and shaking it. Larvae may hibernate in mountain areas. Genetic studies have revealed cryptic lineages, some of which have been attributed to a subspecies, *Lissotriton boscai maltzani*. The species is very common, especially in Portugal, and is not considered threatened.

Identification Criteria
1. One light central crease on the head
2. No dorsal crest in males
3. Bright orange belly
4. Short tail filament in both sexes, and no fringe on hind feet in males

Size: 6–9cm
Habitat: Streams, ditches and ponds with vegetation, in meadows, forests and pastures; up to 1,800m
Reproductive Period: November–June
Sexual Dimorphism: Males are slightly smaller than females; males have a longer filament than females and a large, bulging cloaca (conical in females); ventral side is orange in males, yellow in females
Spawn: As for Smooth Newt (page 122); clutches of 100–250 eggs
Larvae: Similar to Smooth Newt, but up to 5cm long; tail is thin with parallel edges, ending abruptly at the tail tip; olive/yellow coloration with little dark pigmentation
Subspecies: Two (page 200)
IUCN Red List: Least Concern

Left The larvae of the Italian Newt, as with other *Lissotriton*, have large, feathery gills and can reach up to 4cm long.

Italian Newt – *Lissotriton italicus*

This minuscule newt, the smallest in Europe, is easily distinguished from the larger nominate Smooth Newt (the only other small newt present within its range; page 122) by size and other features. It shares a few similarities with the Iberian Bosca's Newt (page 129), including the 'flamenco' move during male courtship and weak sexual dimorphism compared to other species. The Italian Newt inhabits central and southern mainland Italy, where it is quite common, especially at lower elevations.

Identification Criteria
Generally similar to Bosca's Newt but:
① Smaller size
② One light central crease on the head
③ No dorsal crest in males

Size: 5–8cm
Habitat: Small, shallow ponds in sunny situations in lowlands; up to 1,500m
Reproductive Period: November–May
Sexual Dimorphism: As for Bosca's Newt
Spawn: As for Smooth Newt; clutches of 100–250 eggs
Larvae: Generally similar to Smooth Newt; up to 4cm long
IUCN Red List: Least Concern

Left The larvae can be distinguished from that of other small newts by the shape of its tail.

Right Females appear different to males – they are greenish with fewer silver spots.

Alpine Newt – *Ichthyosaura alpestris*

One of the most spectacular newts, the Alpine Newt is a cold-adapted species living up to and above the treeline. It has been moved between genera several times, having been placed originally in *Triturus*, then moved to *Mesotriton* following updates in taxonomy. It is now one of its kind, the only member of the *Ichthyosaura* genus. In lowlands, it can be found together with most other amphibians. Courtship is similar to other small newts, with the male flicking its tail to spread the pheromones emitted by its cloaca. Although locally abundant, this species is threatened in southern parts of its range. It shows a huge diversity, with multiple subspecies and cryptic genetic lineages documented throughout its range.

Identification Criteria
1. Marbled coloration, from green to grey/blue, often with whitish components
2. Spotless, uniform orange belly, even in terrestrial phase
3. No crease on the head
4. No dorsal ridges or tail filament

Size: 7–12cm
Habitat: Mountain ponds, but also woodland areas in lowlands; up to 2,500m
Reproductive Period: March–July
Sexual Dimorphism: Males are slightly smaller than females; males have characteristic marbled coloration with silver spots and a dorsal crest, and a large, bulging cloaca; females have duller coloration (often greenish), smaller spots and a smaller cloaca
Spawn: As for Smooth Newt (page 122); clutches of up to 250 eggs
Larvae: Similar to Smooth Newt but >5cm; tail is thin with parallel edges, ending abruptly in a spike; dark pigmentation
Subspecies: At least six (pages 201–202)
IUCN Red List: Least Concern

Left The eggs of crested and marbled newts are yellowish, and individually deposited on leaves or other aquatic vegetation.

Left During the aquatic phase, males develop a prominent crest – the size and shape of which depends on the species.

Far left Outside the breeding season, individuals undergo a terrestrial phase; marbled newts become brightly coloured.

Salamandridae 2 – Crested and Marbled Newts

Crested and marbled newts (genus *Triturus*) are a species-rich radiation whose evolution and diversity are quite comparable to those of the *Lissotriton vulgaris* species complex (page 122). Different taxa inhabit northern Europe (Great Crested Newt, *T. cristatus*), Iberia (Marbled Newt, *T. marmoratus*; Pygmy Marbled Newt, *T. pygmaeus*), Italy (Italian Crested Newt, *T. carnifex*), the Balkans (Danube Crested Newt, *T. dobrogicus*; Macedonian Crested Newt, *T. macedonicus*; Balkan Crested Newt, *T. ivanbureschi*), Anatolia (Anatolian Crested Newt, *T. anatolicus*) and the Caucasus (Southern Crested Newt, *T. karelinii*).

As in small newts, breeding is aquatic and involves a courtship ritual. The male crested newt bends his back in a 'cat buckle' display, and alternates smooth tail waving with violent tail flicking. He also blocks the path of the female in an almost vertical posture (called the 'brake') during spermatophore transfer, and may bite the female during courtship.

While their large size makes confusion with small newts unlikely, all crested newts are generally similar to each other and only

their distribution guarantees identification. In addition, field specialists measure the ratio of forelimb length to inter-limb length, called the Wolterstorff index (WI), which roughly corresponds to an index of stockiness. However, this morphometric character is not diagnostic for all species and varies between individuals, so a population average needs to be established for the index to be informative. In addition, to complicate things, species hybridise at the margins of their ranges, yielding intermediate values.

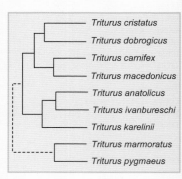

Triturus cristatus
Triturus dobrogicus
Triturus carnifex
Triturus macedonicus
Triturus anatolicus
Triturus ivanbureschi
Triturus karelinii
Triturus marmoratus
Triturus pygmaeus

Left The larvae, bigger than in other newts, bear costal grooves on the flanks.

Right Females have colourful underparts, but lack the dorsal crest.

Great Crested Newt – *Triturus cristatus*

The Great Crested Newt survived the cold of the Quaternary glaciations around the Carpathians, and has since colonised most of northern Europe. In the west of its range it is among the most endangered amphibians, as it requires large, sunny ponds with dense vegetation and unpolluted waters, which are becoming scarce in urbanised western Europe. When threatened, the newt may lie on its back with its eyes closed, playing dead for up to 10 seconds. This widespread species is in contact, and eventually hybridises, with many of its relatives at the periphery of its range.

Identification Criteria
1. Large, slender newt with a prominent crest in males, interrupted between the back and tail
2. Dark with black spots
3. Throat black and yellow with fine white stippling
4. Heavy white stippling on the flanks
5. Belly yellow/orange with irregular black spots
6. WI: male, 0.54–0.64; female, 0.46–0.54

Size: Up to 18cm
Habitat: Large, sunny ponds with dense aquatic vegetation, usually in open landscapes; up to 1,700m
Reproductive Period: April–July
Sexual Dimorphism: Males are smaller than females; males have a dorsal crest and a dark, bulging cloaca; in females, cloaca is flattened and orange
Spawn: Eggs large, yellowish, in oval capsules (larger and different colour from eggs of small newts); 200–400 individually deposited and folded in leaves of aquatic plants
Larvae: 5–8cm; five hind toes; large feathery gills; upper tail fin reaches the back of the head and the tail, pigmented, ending in a filament; 15–16 costal grooves visible on the flanks
IUCN Red List: Least Concern

Left This species is tolerant of many different freshwater habitats.

Right A lack of stippling, but marked spots, are typical of this invasive species.

Italian Crested Newt – *Triturus carnifex*

Naturally present south of the Alps, the Italian Crested Newt is a popular pet among amateur herpetologists. As such, unfortunately it has been released in several places where it does not belong. In western Switzerland and the Netherlands, the species has become invasive and is replacing its Great Crested Newt cousin (page 133). The two species are morphologically similar, although experts can discriminate between them based on differences in their colour patterns. One reason for the species' success appears to be its tolerance for a broad diversity of ponds, even polluted ones.

Identification Criteria
1. Coloration lighter than in Great Crested Newt, with spots more visible
2. Little or no white stippling on the flanks
3. Yellow belly with few large round grey/black spots
4. Dorsal crest lower than in Great Crested Newt and often more denticulate
5. WI: male, 0.62–0.70; female, 0.54–0.64

Size: Up to 18cm
Habitat: Generally similar to Great Crested Newt but found in a broader variety of ponds
Reproductive Period: March–July
Sexual Dimorphism: As for Great Crested Newt
Spawn/Larvae: As for Great Crested Newt
IUCN Red List: Least Concern

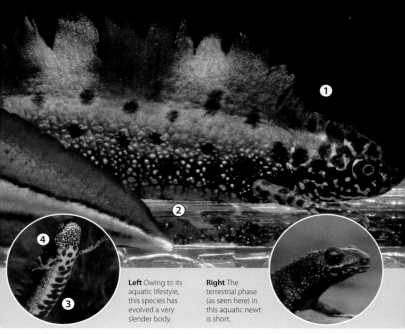

Left Owing to its aquatic lifestyle, this species has evolved a very slender body.

Right The terrestrial phase (as seen here) in this aquatic newt is short.

Danube Crested Newt – *Triturus dobrogicus*

This species inhabits flowing waters and large ponds in the Danube River network and delta. It is also present in the Dnieper River delta in southern Ukraine. As such, the Danube Crested Newt is highly adapted to aquatic life, with a smaller yet more elongated body compared to other crested newts, involving additional rib-bearing vertebrae. The species also has the longest aquatic phase – up to six months – and may even return to water in autumn. The Danube population is severely declining due to habitat destruction and the deterioration of the delta, river and adjacent water systems as a result of pollution, and also due to increased drying of ponds in southern parts of its range as a consequence of global warming.

Identification Criteria
1. Smaller and with a very slender, elongated body compared to other crested newts
2. Heavy white stippling on the flanks
3. Belly deep orange with multiple sharply defined, roundish black spots
4. Throat black with white spots
5. WI: male, 0.38–0.54; female, 0.34–0.46

Size: Up to 13cm
Habitat: River valleys along the Danube water system and its delta, as well as the Dnieper River delta; slow-moving river margins, flooded marshlands, large ponds and ditches with abundant vegetation; up to 600m
Reproductive Period: March–August
Sexual Dimorphism: As for Great Crested Newt (page 133)
Spawn/Larvae: As for Great Crested Newt
IUCN Red List: Near Threatened

Left This species, like its cousin, the Italian Crested Newt, features a light coloration.

Macedonian Crested Newt – *Triturus macedonicus*

The taxonomic position of this newt has changed several times. It used to be considered a subspecies of the former Southern Crested Newt (page 139; which was later split into three distinct species), and then a subspecies of the Italian Crested Newt (page 134). Molecular analyses have confirmed the latter relationship, but support a specific status. Morphologically, the Macedonian Crested Newt is thus very close to the Italian Crested Newt.

Identification Criteria
Generally similar to Italian Crested Newt but:
① Dense white stippling on the flanks
② Belly yellow/orange with irregular small spots

Size: Up to 18cm
Habitat: Various aquatic habitats, including ponds, ditches and marshlands, usually with abundant vegetation
Reproductive Period: April–July
Sexual Dimorphism: As for Great Crested Newt (page 133)
Spawn/Larvae: As for Great Crested Newt
IUCN Red List: —

Left The throat of Asia Minor's *Triturus* newts differs from those found in Europe.

Right This common species is among the most stockily built crested newts.

Anatolian Crested Newt – *Triturus anatolicus*

The Anatolian Crested Newt is a cryptic species, indistinguishable from its relatives the Balkan Crested Newt (page 138) and Southern Crested Newt (page 139), with which it was considered conspecific until the genetic era. These three species are, however, different from other European crested newts, being more stockily built, and lacking a gap between the dorsal and caudal crests in males. They are also semi-aquatic, being terrestrial for most of the year and going back to the water only for breeding. In addition, their genome is bigger than in other *Triturus* species.

Identification Criteria
1. Stocky build, with a less elongated body than most European species
2. Relatively continuous transition between dorsal and caudal crests
3. Throat and belly yellow-orange with many black spots, and without white stippling
4. Wl: male, 0.67–0.82; female, 0.59–0.72

Size: Up to 13cm
Habitat: Various aquatic habitats, including ponds, ditches and marshlands, usually with abundant vegetation
Reproductive Period: February–April
Sexual Dimorphism: As for Great Crested Newt (page 133)
Spawn/Larvae: As for Great Crested Newt
IUCN Red List: —

Left In the aquatic phase, this species, like others from the Balkans and Anatolia, is very colourful.

Balkan Crested Newt – *Triturus ivanbureschi*

This species clearly exemplifies the complex world of newt taxonomy, having been described several times: as the subspecies *Triturus karelinii arntzeni* in 1999, then as the species *T. arntzeni* in 2009. It was then redescribed again in 2013 under a new name, *T. ivanbureschi*, because the former type specimen in fact belonged to a hybrid with the Macedonian Crested Newt (page 136). Indeed, the central Balkans appears to be inhabited by multiple hybridising taxa. The Balkan Crested Newt is present over much of Bulgaria and north-eastern Greece, as well as north-western Anatolia. Some isolated populations also occur in Serbia.

Identification Criteria
Morphologically identical to Anatolian Crested Newt (page 137) and distinguishable only by distribution (see map)

Size: 10–13cm
Habitat: Various aquatic habitats, including ponds, ditches and marshlands, usually with abundant vegetation
Reproductive Period: March–July
Sexual Dimorphism: As for Great Crested Newt (page 133)
Spawn/Larvae: As for Great Crested Newt
IUCN Red List: —

Right In Asia Minor, crested newts have a continuous crest without a gap between the back and the tail.

Southern Crested Newt – *Triturus karelinii*

The range of this large, robust newt was formerly considered to encompass all of northern Anatolia, the Balkans and the Caucasus, but is now restricted to the latter region following taxonomic revisions. Its range also extends to the southern Caspian Sea as well as Crimea, suggesting these areas were connected by marshlands in recent times. In comparison to other crested newts, the species appears to have adapted to more mountainous environments, where it occurs in forest habitats.

Identification Criteria
Morphologically identical to Anatolian Crested Newt (page 137) and distinguishable only by distribution (see map)

Size: Up to 18cm
Habitat: Various aquatic habitats, including ponds, ditches and marshlands, usually with abundant vegetation
Reproductive Period: March–June
Sexual Dimorphism: As for Great Crested Newt (page 133)
Spawn/Larvae: As for Great Crested Newt
IUCN Red List: —

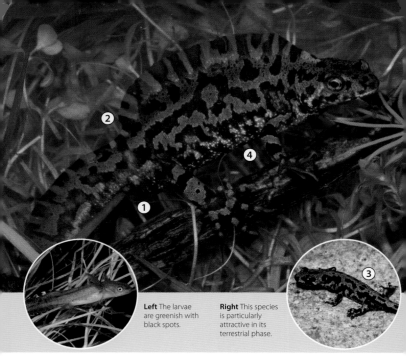

Left The larvae are greenish with black spots.

Right This species is particularly attractive in its terrestrial phase.

Marbled Newt – *Triturus marmoratus*

Marbled Newts inhabit south-western Europe and are the closest relatives of crested newts. As in those species, the male Marbled Newt bears a crest during the aquatic phase. In north-western France, Marbled Newts sometimes hybridise with the Great Crested Newt (page 133), yielding offspring of intermediate coloration and morphotype that used to be erroneously assigned to a different species (described as *Triturus blasii*). Some experimental studies have suggested that Marbled Newts may use celestial cues (the position of stars in the sky) to orientate towards breeding sites.

Identification Criteria
1. Attractive, marbled green and black camouflage pattern
2. Relatively undulated and barred dorsal crest in breeding males, reduced at tail base
3. Orange/red dorsal line in terrestrial phase (also in aquatic phase for female)
4. Dark/greyish belly with white spots
5. Stocky build. WI: male, 0.70–0.80; female, 0.62–0.74

Size: Up to 16cm
Habitat: Diverse habitats in hilly landscapes, including ponds, ditches and streams
Reproductive Period: March–August in France, November–June in Spain and Portugal
Sexual Dimorphism: Females are generally larger; in the aquatic phase, males have a dorsal crest, white lines on the tail edges and a large, bulging cloaca; females keep their orange dorsal line instead of developing a crest
Spawn: As for Great Crested Newt
Larvae: Generally similar to Great Crested Newt but with only 12–13 costal grooves, light greenish coloration and black spots, especially on the tail fin
IUCN Red List: Least Concern

Left This attractive species has a marbled green coloration with black blotches.

Right This species is threatened by the drainage of ponds, associated with intensive agriculture.

Pygmy Marbled Newt – *Triturus pygmaeus*

The Pygmy Marbled Newt is a dwarf version of the Marbled Newt (page 140), of which it was considered a subspecies until recently. The two have similar courtship rituals to crested newts, but in addition the male may erotically bite the female and hold her for several minutes. The species' range is parapatric, roughly separated by the Douro–Tagus watershed in central Portugal and Spain. The hybrid zone between them is moving northward due to the warming of the climate since the last glaciation. This species is threatened by the drainage of ponds associated with intensive agriculture.

Identification Criteria
Similar to Marbled Newt but:
① Smaller in size
② Belly often yellow or whitish with dark spots

Size: Up to 12cm
Habitat: Temperate and Mediterranean forests with rivers, marshes, ponds and other water bodies
Reproductive Period: October–May
Sexual Dimorphism: As for Marbled Newt
Spawn/Larvae: As for Marbled Newt
IUCN Red List: Near Threatened

Left Brightly coloured *Neurergus* are found in localised areas in Turkey and Iran.

Above and left Eggs are often grouped together on stones or vegetation (above). *Ommatotriton* have spectacular crests and colourful flank patterns.

Salamandridae 3 – Banded and Spotted Newts

Banded and spotted newts, from the genera *Ommatotriton* and *Neurergus* respectively, are spectacular amphibians inhabiting the Middle East. They were formerly grouped with other newts under the genus *Triturus*, before complete reclassification in the 2000s.

Ommatotriton males have a massive spiky crest. They are territorial and very aggressive: they will fight each other to guard their spot in the pond, sometimes until death. An encounter with a female is followed by the courtship ritual, which generally resembles that of *Triturus* newts. Three species exist, with different distributions: Northern Banded Newt (*O. ophryticus*) around the south-eastern shores of the Black Sea; Nesterov's Banded Newt (*O. nesterovi*) in north-western Anatolia; and Southern Banded Newt (*O. vittatus*) in the Levant region.

Spotted newts (*Neurergus*) are colourful species that inhabit mountain streams in the Middle East, mainly in Turkey, Iran and surrounding areas. Apart from Kaiser's Spotted Newt (*N. kaiseri*), they are black with yellow spots. They are highly threatened due to their restricted distribution as well as frequent harvesting

for the pet trade, and not much is known about their biology in the wild. Spotted newts breed in streams during the rainy season at the beginning of the calendar year. As their natural habitats are dry outside this period, they aestivate in nearby woodland for the rest of the year. In addition to the classical waving and whipping features, their courtship ritual involves the brake position (as in crested and marbled newts, pages 132–41). Females of some species (Kaiser's Spotted Newt and Strauch's Spotted Newt) also adopt the flamenco position after spermatophore pick-up, holding their tail up and stretching it.

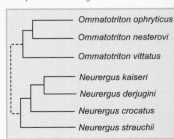

Ommatotriton ophryticus
Ommatotriton nesterovi
Ommatotriton vittatus
Neurergus kaiseri
Neurergus derjugini
Neurergus crocatus
Neurergus strauchii

Left Larvae resemble those of crested newts, but are slender and lack costal grooves.

Right Females are much more distinct than males, lacking the dorsal crests.

Northern Banded Newt – *Ommatotriton ophryticus*

This species is very popular in herpetologists' terrariums. Extremely attractive, it is difficult to confuse with other *Lissotriton* and *Triturus* species with which it might be found. The Northern Banded Newt is declining due to anthropogenic pressures such as deforestation, cattle overgrazing and the introduction of alien fish, and predation by invasive Raccoons (*Procyon lotor*) in the Caucasus. It is also harvested for the pet trade. In the aquatic phase, the adult eats various invertebrates, as well as the eggs of other amphibians, including those of conspecifics.

Identification Criteria
1. Narrow silver-white and black bands on the flanks
2. Very high, spiky dorsal crest in males (up to 3cm)
3. Denticulation of the lower edge of the tail
4. Greenish-blue flash on the tail in males
5. Orange belly, usually spotless

Size: 9–13cm

Habitat: Different kinds of forests up to subalpine meadows, in lakes, ponds, puddles, canals and ditches; up to 2,700m

Reproductive Period: March–July

Sexual Dimorphism: Males are slightly bigger than females; males have a high, spiky crest, flashy colour patterns and a bulging cloaca; females lack the crest and have dull coloration

Spawn: Eggs yellowish; 50–200 deposited singly or in short chains under rocks or vegetation, at a depth of 5–30cm

Larvae: Up to 7cm; golden base colour with dark pigmentation; large feathery gills; elongated body without costal grooves; parallel tail fins ending in a pointy tip

IUCN Red List: —

Left The tail of males features a very bright blue streak.

Nesterov's Banded Newt – *Ommatotriton nesterovi*

Originally described as a subspecies of the Northern Banded Newt (page 143), Nesterov's Banded Newt was elevated to species status based on its differing number of trunk vertebrae and genome size. Recent genetic data have further suggested all three banded newts diverged as a result of mountain formation in Anatolia, following the collision between the Arabian and Eurasian tectonic plates.

Identification Criteria
Morphologically identical to Northern Banded Newt and distinguishable only by distribution (see map)

Size: 9–12cm
Habitat: As for Northern Banded Newt
Reproductive Period: March–July
Sexual Dimorphism: As for Northern Banded Newt
Spawn/Larvae: As for Northern Banded Newt
IUCN Red List: —

Left Males of this species can be very colourful.

Right During courtship, males diffuse pheromones by tail movements.

Southern Banded Newt – *Ommatotriton vittatus*

The third species of banded newt is smaller than the others and is found in south-eastern Anatolia and the Levant region, which are inhabited by two different subspecies. As in other newts, predators include grass snakes and marsh frogs, as well as birds such as crows. The Southern Banded Newt appears to be less restricted by aridity compared to its cousins. Males develop their crests after entering breeding waters. The breeding behaviour is similar to that of the other banded newts, with close encounters between males resulting in fierce struggles.

Identification Criteria
Generally similar to Northern Banded Newt (page 143) but:
① Smaller in size
② Often has small dark spots on the ventral side

Size: 8–10cm
Habitat: As for Northern Banded Newt
Reproductive Period: January–February in the Levant; until June in Anatolia
Sexual Dimorphism: As for Northern Banded Newt
Spawn/Larvae: As for Northern Banded Newt
Subspecies: Two (page 202)
IUCN Red List: Least Concern

Left This attractive species is highly threatened by the pet trade.

Right The appearance of the larvae hints at the future adult coloration.

Kaiser's Spotted Newt – *Neurergus kaiseri*

Kaiser's Spotted Newt, also known as the Emperor Spotted Newt, is a magnificent yet enigmatic amphibian known from only four remote highland streams in the southern Zagros Mountains in Lorestan province, Iran. Much of its natural history is still unknown. Several captive breeding programmes involving zoos worldwide aim at preserving the species, whose numbers severely declined following collection for the pet trade and droughts in the past two decades. With fewer than 10,000 wild breeding individuals remaining, it was the first species granted international protection from e-commerce, and its import and export are banned by CITES, the Convention on International Trade in Endangered Species.

Identification Criteria
1. Small newt with a flattened head
2. Spectacular black, white and orange coloration
3. Long, narrow orange dorsal stripe
4. Belly uniform orange

Size: 11–14cm
Habitat: Spring-fed mountain streams in arid shrubland habitats, usually in slow-flowing parts with a sandy substrate, as well as nearby pools; Shahbazan, Taleh Zang, Hajbarikab, Shahzade Ahmad river valleys; altitudes of 750–2,000m
Reproductive Period: March–April
Sexual Dimorphism: Females are slightly larger than males; females have a fleshy protuberance on the cloaca at the tail base; males have a bulging cloaca and lack the protuberance
Spawn: Eggs small (4mm with capsule); small clutches (40–60 eggs), deposited singly on rocks in riverbeds, sometimes on aquatic vegetation
Larvae: Small (up to 5cm); yellow with black spots when young, light spots forming rows on the back when older; tail lacks pigmentation and has a high upper fin reaching past the middle of the body
IUCN Red List: Vulnerable

Left Eggs are often deposited together under rocks.

Right This largely aquatic species is found in cool mountain streams.

Strauch's Spotted Newt – *Neurergus strauchii*

Slender and larger than Kaiser's Spotted Newt (page 146), this species is known from remote areas of eastern Anatolia. Although it is locally abundant, it is threatened by water pollution and habitat loss. It was named after Alexander Strauch (1832–93), a Russian herpetologist. Dark with tiny yellow spots, its skin is not glossy as that of salamanders in the genus *Salamandra*.

Identification Criteria
① Granular black skin with many small yellow/orange spots
② Orange part of belly is limited to a narrow line

Size: 16–19cm
Habitat: Small, cool mountain streams in shrubland, often without vegetation; altitudes of 1,000–2,000m
Reproductive Period: May–April
Sexual Dimorphism: Females have a slightly conical cloaca; males have a bulging cloaca and their tail spots can develop a silver-blue colour
Spawn: Eggs 5–6mm in diameter (with capsule); clutches of 70–110 deposited under river stones individually or in clumps joined by jelly strings
Larvae: Up to 7cm, with short gills; grey when young, developing light spots in rows on the back and belly with age; tail has dark pigmentation, and upper tail fin reaches no further than the middle of the body; tail tip rounded
Subspecies: Three (page 203)
IUCN Red List: Vulnerable

Left Some populations feature large yellow blotches on its black skin, however, this is quite variable.

Azerbaijan Newt – *Neurergus crocatus*

Found in the mountains west of Iran's Lake Urmia, from which it gets its alternative name of Lake Urmia Newt, this species exhibits different spotted morphotypes depending on the population, which might reflect distinct evolutionary histories. Originally described from the former Iranian province of Azerbaijan (hence its name) in 1862, the newt was later thought extinct from the area and persists only in other parts of north-western Iran, north-eastern Iraq and south-eastern Turkey. The construction of dams will likely threaten this stream-breeding species.

Identification Criteria
Generally similar to Strauch's Spotted Newt (page 147) but:
① Fewer but larger yellow blotches

Size: 16–18cm
Habitat: Mountain streams with small ponds and waterfalls
Reproductive Period: March–April
Sexual Dimorphism: Breeding females have a slightly protruding cloaca and yellow ventral side; males have a bulging cloaca and orange-red ventral side; breeding males have large, shiny white dots aligned on the tail
Spawn: Eggs large (up to 9mm with capsule); clutches of 150–200 eggs, joined by a jelly string, are deposited on or under river stones
Larvae: Generally similar to Strauch's Spotted Newt, but upper tail fin reaches beyond the middle of the body; older larvae have bright blotches and variable tail pigmentation
IUCN Red List: Vulnerable

Left This black and yellow newt is conspicuous in the mountain streams it inhabits

Right Older larvae already feature spotted patterns.

Kurdistan Newt – *Neurergus derjugini*

A very localised species, the Kurdistan Newt is now restricted to just four streams in the Zagros Mountains in Iran, with an uncertain presence in Iraq and Turkey. Like other members of the genus *Neurergus*, this species is a stream-breeder whose females deposit their eggs in the water. It is extremely threatened as a result of recent droughts and water pollution by pesticides; the next few years may be the last chance to see the species before it becomes extinct, unless conservation measures are undertaken. In older taxonomies it was named *Neurergus microspilotus*.

Identification Criteria
Generally similar to Strauch's Spotted Newt (page 147) but:
① Cloaca shapes differ (see 'Sexual Dimorphism')
② Multiple dorsal blotches of variable size and numbers

Size: 15–17cm
Habitat: Shallow, clear streams in mountainous areas; altitudes of 1,200–1,800m
Reproductive Period: April–June
Sexual Dimorphism: Females are slightly larger than males; breeding males have a protruding semicircular cloaca; females have a tubular cloaca (3cm in length)
Spawn: Eggs 6mm long with capsule; clutches of 100 eggs laid in clumps or individually on vegetation and rocks in the stream bed
Larvae: Generally similar to Strauch's Spotted Newt, but belly spots are usually dark in older larvae
IUCN Red List: Critically Endangered

Left and below *Euproctus* and *Calotriton* have flat and elongated bodies, adapted to swimming in fast-flowing streams.

Left The Iberian Ribbed Newt is actually the only ribbed newt bearing rib tubercles along its body.

Salamandridae 4 – Brook and Ribbed Newts

This section regroups different kinds of Caudata endemic to the western Mediterranean region: the brook newts, inhabiting mountain streams in the Pyrenees (genus *Calotriton*) and highland brooks in Corsica and Sardinia (genus *Euproctus*); and the ribbed newts, which have colonised the dry lands of southern Iberia and North Africa (genus *Pleurodeles*).

With their flattened head and body, *Calotriton* species were long considered close to *Euproctus*, but they are in fact cousins of the crested newts (*Triturus*). The adaptation of *Calotriton* to fast-running oxygenated mountain streams has led to the rapid evolution of traits superficially similar to those in *Euproctus*, a process known as evolutionary convergence. The two *Calotriton* species have localised distributions: the Pyrenean Newt (*C. asper*) occurs throughout the Pyrenees; and the Montseny Newt (*C. arnoldi*) is found in the Catalan pre-coastal range.

Euproctus species are interchangeably called mountain newts or brook salamanders. Largely aquatic, the two species – found in Corsica (Corsican Mountain Newt, *E. montanus*) and Sardinia

(Sardinian Mountain Newt, *E. platycephalus*) – have no lungs and instead breathe only through their skin. In both *Calotriton* and *Euproctus*, courtship is quite different from other newts: the male displays his coloured underparts, before grasping an interested female with his tail and transferring his spermatophore directly into her cloaca.

Ribbed newts are so-called owing to the sharp ribs that protrude through lateral tubercles in the sides of the nominal species, the Iberian Ribbed Newt (*Pleurodeles waltl*). These rib tips might be part of a primitive defence system: the stinging tubercles secrete toxins as the newt moves, thus acting as potential poisonous anti-predator 'fences'.

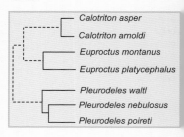

- Calotriton asper
- Calotriton arnoldi
- Euproctus montanus
- Euproctus platycephalus
- Pleurodeles waltl
- Pleurodeles nebulosus
- Pleurodeles poireti

Left Larvae can be found in mountain streams and ponds, where they may overwinter.

Right Direct contact avoids spermatophores being swept away by the current.

Pyrenean Newt – *Calotriton asper*

This stream-breeder occurs as isolated populations in several river systems in the Pyrenees. Largely aquatic, Pyrenean Newts stay in the water from spring to autumn as long as temperatures are above 5–6°C. In lowlands, they aestivate under terrestrial rocks during the summer, when water temperatures get too warm. Some cave-dwelling populations remain aquatic year-round, but their reproductive period is longer as it is disturbed due to the lack of light. At altitude, larvae often overwinter and can grow large. Mainly nocturnal, the newt often hides under rocks in the calm parts of streams. Trout are its main predators.

Identification Criteria
1. Sturdy body with a flattened head
2. Body covered with warts
3. No parotoid gland
4. No crest in breeding males
5. Dull back coloration, with flashy yellowish dorsal stripe sometimes present, especially in young individuals
6. Belly yellow to red in colour

Size: 8–14cm
Habitat: Clear, fresh, oxygenated waters in mountain streams and adjoining ponds and lakes, sometimes caves, usually with scarce or absent vegetation; up to 2,500m
Reproductive Period: February–May; usually initiated by snowmelt
Sexual Dimorphism: Females are usually larger than males; females have a conical cloaca with a small backward-oriented tube; males have a rounded cloaca
Spawn: Eggs whitish, 4–6mm in diameter with capsule; 20–40 laid annually, deposited individually under rocks or in rock interstices
Larvae: Grows to 8–9cm at altitude (overwintering); elongated body with short gills; short upper tail fin reaching about one-third of the way along the back; tail tip rounded
IUCN Red List: Near Threatened

Left The brownish colour of this species is ideal for mimicry in rocky and leafy streams.

Montseny Newt – *Calotriton arnoldi*

First described in 2005, the Montseny Newt is endemic to the mountains of the same name in Catalonia, north-eastern Spain. It differs from the Pyrenean Newt (page 151) genetically and in some morphological features, such as its shorter length, the shape of the vertebrae at the base of the tail and skin texture. When handled, the newt releases an odorous, sticky skin secretion. Its brownish skin coloration may serve a mimetic function, being similar to Beech (*Fagus sylvatica*) leaves. Found in only low numbers along seven streams in two areas of the Montseny Natural Park, this species is of high conservation concern.

Identification Criteria
Generally similar to Pyrenean Newt but:
① Smaller and with smoother skin
② Chocolate-brown coloration
③ Dorsal stripe dull brownish, never flashy

Size: 8–10cm
Habitat: Cold, fast-running waters in Beech and Holm Oak (*Quercus ilex*) forests in the Montseny Mountains; altitudes of 600–1,200m
Reproductive Period: No data, but probably March–May given its altitudinal range
Sexual Dimorphism: Similar to Pyrenean Newt, but no size dimorphism
Spawn/Larvae: Poorly known, but probably similar to Pyrenean Newt
IUCN Red List: Critically Endangered

Left This species has very prominent parotoid glands.

Right Although this species is aquatic, it can be seen outside the water.

Corsican Mountain Newt – *Euproctus montanus*

A cryptic inhabitant of Corsican mountain streams, this small species is mainly nocturnal and can be found only by flipping over river stones. Yet it is relatively common, especially at middle altitudes. During breeding, the male holds the female with his overdeveloped jaws and uses spurs on his hind feet to stimulate her. Copulation lasts up to four hours. The male has a pseudopenis in his cloaca, which facilitates direct spermatophore transfer. After spawning, the female subsequently guards the breeding site to protect her eggs, sometimes in cooperation with other females.

Identification Criteria
1. Small aquatic newt with a flattened body
2. Parotoid glands visible
3. Smooth, weakly granular skin
4. Variable coloration

Size: 8–10cm, sometimes up to 13cm
Habitat: Fast-running oxygenated streams and connected pools in open areas of the Corsican maquis, as well as chestnut forests; up to 2,200m, but abundant at 600–1,500m
Reproductive Period: March–June and September–October in lowlands; June–August at high altitude
Sexual Dimorphism: Males have a larger head (with more developed jaws), spurs on the hindlimbs, and a conical cloaca that projects backwards; females have a swollen hemispherical cloaca
Spawn: 20–40 eggs are laid per year, deposited individually underneath river rocks
Larvae: Up to 5cm; small head and elongated body with short gills; tail fin short and spotless, reaching the posterior limbs; tail tip rounded
IUCN Red List: Least Concern

Left A small head with short gills and an elongated body are typical of the larvae.

Right This species has a flatter and more pointed head than its Corsican relative.

Sardinian Mountain Newt – *Euproctus platycephalus*

The scientific species name *platycephalus* is Greek for 'flat head', a characteristic feature of this Sardinian endemic, which unlike its Corsican Mountain Newt cousin (page 153) has discreet parotoid glands. It inhabits calm parts of streams in mountain areas, and can also be found on nearby land under roots, dead wood or stones. Highly threatened, the Sardinian Mountain Newt has disappeared from many localities, notably due to the use of antimalarial pesticides in the twentieth century, as well as predation by, and competition from, trout introduced for recreational fishing.

Identification Criteria
Similar to Corsican Mountain Newt but:
① Less distinct parotoid glands
② More flattened and elongated head

Size: 10–14cm
Habitat: Mountain rivers and small lakes, especially relatively calm streams; up to 1,800m, but more abundant above 600m
Reproductive Period: April–May and September–October; only during the summer in high altitudes
Sexual Dimorphism: Males are slightly bigger than females; males have a larger head (with more developed jaws), as well as spurs on the hindlimbs; both sexes have a conical, hook-shaped cloaca
Spawn: Eggs whitish; up to 200 laid annually, deposited individually in stone cavities via the elongated cloaca
Larvae: Similar to Corsican Mountain Newt but the upper tail fin is higher and extends up to the middle of the body
IUCN Red List: Endangered

Left Some individuals can appear paler, especially in sandy habitats.

Right The warts on the side are presumably used to secrete toxins as a defence.

Iberian Ribbed Newt – *Pleurodeles waltl*

The largest of the European Caudata, the Iberian Ribbed Newt is also one of the most famous. It is a model organism for the study of regeneration, since, like some other salamanders, it can regrow limbs and regenerate injured brain, heart, eye lens and spinal cord tissues. The species was also sent into space on several missions to study the effects of microgravity. During breeding, the mating pair swims together while hugging (sometimes for up to 48 hours), during which several spermatophores are released and absorbed by the female. The Iberian Ribbed Newt is significantly declining due to habitat loss and predation of its eggs and larvae by invasive Red Swamp Crayfish (*Procambarus clarkii*).

Identification Criteria
1. Very large newt with variable brownish coloration
2. Large, flattened head
3. 8–10 rounded whitish or yellowish-orange warty spots along the sides (rib tips)

Size: 17–30cm

Habitat: Various Mediterranean lowland biotopes, including meadows, cultivated land and shrubland with temporary ponds, usually with abundant vegetation; up to 1,500m

Reproductive Period: November–January

Sexual Dimorphism: Males are slightly bigger than females; breeding males have dark nuptial pads in the inner sides of the forelimbs

Spawn: Eggs 6–7mm with capsule; up to 800 deposited over the space of a few days in clumps of 10–20, attached to plants or stones

Larvae: Up to 8cm; large feathery gills; high upper tail fin, starting from the head and ending in a fine tail tip; head large with small eyes and a rounded snout

IUCN Red List: Near Threatened

Left Note the absence of rib tips (compared with Iberian Ribbed Newt).

Algerian Ribbed Newt – *Pleurodeles nebulosus*

Despite its common name and unlike the Iberian Ribbed Newt (page 155), the Algerian Ribbed Newt lacks protruding rib tips. Inhabiting a restricted range along the Tunisian and Algerian coast, it is also considerably smaller than its cousin (which is found in Morocco as well as Iberia) and differs in the number of vertebrae. It is threatened by landscape changes involving agricultural development and grazing by livestock. Before the start of the twenty-first century, it was called *Pleurodeles poireti*, which actually corresponds to an endemic species restricted to the Edough Peninsula (page 157).

Identification Criteria
Similar to Iberian Ribbed Newt but:
① Smaller in size
② Rib tips absent

Size: 10–18cm
Habitat: Diverse aquatic habitats, including rivers, swamps and marshes; up to 1,000m
Reproductive Period: November–February
Sexual Dimorphism: Females are slightly larger than males, although the tail in males is longer than their body (shorter in females); breeding males have a swollen cloaca and reddish-brown nuptial pads on the inner side of the forelimbs
Spawn/Larvae: As for Iberian Ribbed Newt
IUCN Red List: Vulnerable

Right This species is endemic to the Edough Peninsula in north-eastern Algeria, where it can be found in the massif of the same name.

Edough Ribbed Newt – *Pleurodeles poireti*

This poorly known species is restricted to the Edough Peninsula in Numidia, northern Algeria. It split from the Algerian Ribbed Newt (page 156) four million years ago, during periods when sea levels rose and the peninsula was an island. Genetic data and the newt's significantly smaller size supported its recognition as a different species. The shape of the row of palatine teeth is also different (V-shaped in Edough Ribbed Newt and U-shaped in Algerian Ribbed Newt), although this is not easy to assess in the field.

Identification Criteria
(1) A dwarf form of Algerian Ribbed Newt
(2) Narrower head and shorter limbs than Algerian Ribbed Newt

Size: 9–13cm
Habitat: Rivers, swamps, marshes and ponds on the Edough Peninsula; up to 800m
Reproductive Period: November–February
Sexual Dimorphism: Similar to Algerian Ribbed Newt, but with more accentuated size differences
Spawn/Larvae: Supposedly similar to both Algerian Ribbed Newt and Iberian Ribbed Newt (page 155)
IUCN Red List: Endangered

Salamandridae 5 – True Salamanders

In contrast with newts, salamanders are mainly terrestrial animals. They breed on land and most species rely on aquatic habitats at the larval stage only. Reproductive behaviour and strategies are quite variable. Mating usually takes place with the male carrying the female on his back, a position called ventral amplexus. He stimulates her with his tail and releases a spermatophore on the ground, then positions the female so that she can absorb it with her cloaca. In *Salamandrina*, courtship is different and does not involve physical contact between partners. Some salamander taxa lay eggs, while others give birth to larvae (larviparous) or even fully formed juveniles (viviparous).

Salamandra species inhabit forest areas, from lowlands to mountains. They are usually nocturnal and quite discreet, but are worth finding. Most display spectacular colours, with strong regional variation that has led to the description of many subspecies. Beautiful but deadly, salamanders are famous for their toxicity: they produce different alkaloid toxins, including samandarine, which can be lethal at high concentrations.

True salamanders include the genera *Salamandra*, *Chioglossa*, *Mertensiella*, *Salamandrina* and *Lyciasalamandra*. The latter is a complex of seven extremely localised species from south-western Anatolia (Lycia), and is treated separately in the next section (Salamandridae 6; pages 170–77).

The genus *Salamandra* currently includes six species, which are predominantly glossy black with a variable amount of yellow or red coloration. These are the widespread Common Fire Salamander (*S. salamandra*) in central and western Europe; the more localised Corsican Fire Salamander (*S. corsica*; Corsica), North African Fire Salamander (*S. algira*; North Africa) and Near Eastern Fire Salamander (*S. infraimmaculata*; Middle East); as well as the Alpine Salamander (*S. atra*) and Lanza's Alpine Salamander (*S. lanzai*), both resident in the Alps.

The very slender Golden-striped Salamander (*Chioglossa lusitanica*) and Caucasian Salamander (*Mertensiella caucasica*) are the only representatives of

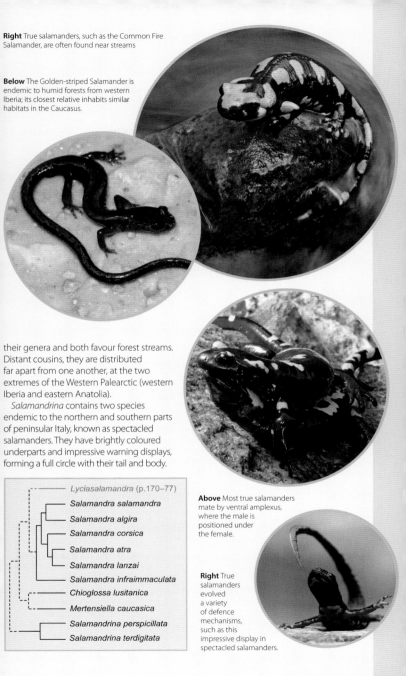

Right True salamanders, such as the Common Fire Salamander, are often found near streams

Below The Golden-striped Salamander is endemic to humid forests from western Iberia; its closest relative inhabits similar habitats in the Caucasus.

their genera and both favour forest streams. Distant cousins, they are distributed far apart from one another, at the two extremes of the Western Palearctic (western Iberia and eastern Anatolia).

Salamandrina contains two species endemic to the northern and southern parts of peninsular Italy, known as spectacled salamanders. They have brightly coloured underparts and impressive warning displays, forming a full circle with their tail and body.

Lyciasalamandra (p.170–77)
Salamandra salamandra
Salamandra algira
Salamandra corsica
Salamandra atra
Salamandra lanzai
Salamandra infraimmaculata
Chioglossa lusitanica
Mertensiella caucasica
Salamandrina perspicillata
Salamandrina terdigitata

Above Most true salamanders mate by ventral amplexus, where the male is positioned under the female.

Right True salamanders evolved a variety of defence mechanisms, such as this impressive display in spectacled salamanders.

Left Many subspecies have been described, including *S. s. fastuosa.*

Right Larvae of this species are commonly found in calm stream puddles.

Common Fire Salamander – *Salamandra salamandra*

Spotting this emblematic animal during a forest hike is always a fine surprise. Common Fire Salamanders spend much of their time under rocks and leaves or around mossy tree trunks, becoming active at dusk and at night, and especially during rainy days. This species shows remarkable variability in reproductive strategies: females are often larviparous (giving birth to larvae), but they are viviparous in some populations/subspecies (giving birth to fully formed juveniles), probably as an adaptation to dry environments that lack water bodies. A unique behaviour of fire salamanders is their capacity to spray poison actively from their dorsal glands when under attack.

Identification Criteria
1. Large, strong salamander
2. Prominent parotoid glands
3. Smooth, glossy black skin with yellow patches, although there is great variability in colour patterns between subspecies

Size: 13–22cm
Habitat: Deciduous forests with small brooks or ponds with clean water; up to 2,100m, but commonly found below 1,000m
Reproductive Period: March–September
Sexual Dimorphism: The sexes are similar, but breeding males have a swollen cloaca
Spawn/Larvae: No egg is laid; after 6–8 months of gestation, the female gives birth to up to 70 small larvae (usually 2–3cm long); the larvae have a large head, rounded snout and short gills, and an elongated body with a short upper tail fin reaching one-third of the way along the back; old larvae are spotted and usually reach 7cm long (9cm in *Salamandra salamandra almonzoris*); viviparity is known in *S. s. bernardezi* and *S. s. fastuosa*, and sometimes in *S. s. salamandra*
Subspecies: Fourteen (pages 204–206)
IUCN Red List: Least Concern

Left This species is often found in mountain streams in the Corsican Maquis.

Right In dry areas, the Corsican Fire Salamander can be viviparous.

Corsican Fire Salamander – *Salamandra corsica*

Another amphibian endemic to Corsica, this species was once considered one of the numerous subspecies of the Common Fire Salamander (page 160). It differs in some morphological features, but most importantly in its strong genetic divergence: it is, in fact, more closely related to the alpine salamanders. While most females lay larvae, some are viviparous, probably because many parts of the island lack suitable water bodies. Categorised as Least Concern by the IUCN, the Corsican Fire Salamander nevertheless faces threats from habitat destruction, wildfires and predation by invasive fish.

Identification Criteria
Similar to Common Fire Salamander but:
① Parotoid glands well defined but relatively small
② Yellow patches randomly distributed

Size: Up to 20cm
Habitat: Humid patches of deciduous and mixed forests in the maquis, sometimes in caves; up to 1,700m
Reproductive Period: March–June and September–October in lowlands; June–August at high altitude
Sexual Dimorphism: As for Common Fire Salamander
Spawn/Larvae: As for Common Fire Salamander; larviparous, with occasional cases of viviparity
IUCN Red List: Least Concern

Left Note the yellow and red patches on the head.

Right The viviparous subspecies *S. s. tingitana* is almost entirely black.

North African Fire Salamander – *Salamandra algira*

Another former subspecies of the Common Fire Salamander (page 160), the North African Fire Salamander occurs in isolated patches from Morocco to Algeria, where different subspecies occur. The name fire salamander is actually a tautology, since salamander derives from the Greek words meaning 'fire lizard'. It originates from an old legend that salamanders can withstand fire: often sheltering in damp logs, they would crawl out uninjured when the logs were thrown into wood fires. In fact, this legend is partly true: under stress, salamanders coat their bodies with a mucus-like venom, which might protect them from burn injuries – at least during the time they make their escape.

Identification Criteria
(1) More slender than other fire salamanders
(2) Variable amount of irregular yellow patches and red spots, notably on the head

Size: 18–24cm
Habitat: Humid mountain forests and mixed woodlands, with shallow, small water bodies such as streams and ponds for breeding; up to 2,400m
Reproductive Period: November–May
Sexual Dimorphism: As for Common Fire Salamander
Spawn/Larvae: As for Common Fire Salamander; females give birth to 15–20 relatively advanced larvae (3.5cm at birth); subspecies are mostly larviparous except the viviparous *Salamandra algira tingitana*
Subspecies: Four (page 206)
IUCN Red List: Vulnerable

Left The nominal subspecies (seen here) has large yellow patches on the head.

Right The easternmost populations feature tiny yellow dots.

Near Eastern Fire Salamander – *Salamandra infraimmaculata*

The largest species in the genus *Salamandra*, the Near Eastern Fire Salamander inhabits coastal to mountainous forests from south-eastern Anatolia to Israel, where it is threatened by habitat destruction. The species breeds during the coolest months of the year, although the subspecies *S. infraimmaculata orientalis* and *S. i. semenovi*, which are restricted to high altitudes, are active during the summer months. It is entirely terrestrial, with only the females making brief visits to water in order to deposit their larvae. The Near Eastern Fire Salamander is threatened by pesticide pollution, predation by introduced fish and habitat destruction, notably the damming of breeding streams.

Identification Criteria
Similar to Common Fire Salamander (page 160) but:
① Larger size

Size: Up to 32cm
Habitat: Dry subtropical shrubland and humid mountain forests, with freshwater brooks and temporary pools; up to 2,000m
Reproductive Period: November–March in the lowlands; April–July in the highlands
Sexual Dimorphism: As for Common Fire Salamander; females are usually larger than males
Spawn/Larvae: As for Common Fire Salamander; mostly larviparous, but viviparity reported in Turkey
Subspecies: Three (page 207)
IUCN Red List: Near Threatened

Left Subspecies *S. a. aurorae* shows continuous yellow coloration on the back.

Right Subspecies *S. a. pasubiensis*, from the Pasubio Massif, features tiny yellow dots.

Alpine Salamander – *Salamandra atra*

Finding an Alpine Salamander is always a fine reward after turning over dozens of rocks during a mountain hike. Although cryptic, the species can be very abundant: up to 2,000 individuals per hectare have been recorded in some locations. This species is exclusively viviparous, the females giving birth to fully formed young after a long gestation period (up to three years at high altitudes). Thus, it does not depend on water for reproduction and is completely terrestrial. That said, individuals are quite stationary: in a capture–recapture study, the maximum observed distance travelled during an entire summer was 12m. Two localised subspecies display yellow pattern coloration.

Identification Criteria
1. Medium-sized salamander
2. Uniform glossy black coloration (nominate form)
3. Tail tip pointy

Size: 9–14cm
Habitat: Alpine and subalpine meadows and forest undergrowth; altitudes of 500–3,000m
Reproductive Period: May– August; once the snow has thawed
Sexual Dimorphism: Males are slightly smaller than females and have a swollen cloaca
Spawn/Larvae: Viviparous; females give birth to two to four juveniles per gestation
Subspecies: Three (page 208)
IUCN Red List: Least Concern

Left This shy salamander hides in the alpine grass very close to mountain streams.

Right This species is larger than *S. atra* and its tail tip is rounded.

Lanza's Alpine Salamander – *Salamandra lanzai*

A mountain salamander restricted at the French–Italian border in the western Piedmont Alps, this species is named after Italian herpetologist Benedetto Lanza (1924–2016). Viviparous like the Alpine Salamander (page 164), it differs from that species in both morphological and genetic features. Females give birth to up to six juveniles after up to four years of gestation. Lanza's Alpine Salamander is poisonous, thanks to a row of glandular protuberances on its sides. Although it faces no current major risks, except from cars on roads, its restricted range makes it susceptible to threat.

Identification Criteria
Similar to Alpine Salamander but:
1. Larger size
2. Longer tail, ending in a rounded tip in adults
3. Flatter head
4. Slight webbing between fingers and toes

Size: 11–17cm
Habitat: Subalpine and alpine meadows with rocks, near mountainous streams; altitudes of 1,200–2,600m
Reproductive Period: May–October
Sexual Dimorphism: Males have a more prominent, swollen cloaca than females
Spawn/Larvae: Viviparous; females give birth to two to six juveniles per gestation
IUCN Red List: Vulnerable

Left This species is found in rich undergrowth in forests, close to mountain streams.

Right Most of the range is inhabited by *C. l. longipes*, which features longer limbs.

Golden-striped Salamander – *Chioglossa lusitanica*

Threatened due to its specific habitat requirements (clean mountain streams in humid forests), this species is nevertheless quite widespread and abundant in Portugal and into north-west Spain. As in *Salamandra*, mating pairs form ventral amplexus, although unlike many salamandrids, females are oviparous, laying eggs. When in danger, the Golden-striped Salamander can break off its tail, which will continue to move in order to distract predators. The salamander regenerates its tail, but loses the fat reserves stored in the original, which in turn reduces fecundity in females. Larvae are fully nocturnal and can overwinter up to three years.

Identification Criteria
1. Very slender salamander with a long tail (two-thirds of its total length)
2. Copper-coloured bands run along the back and tail
3. Small head with large, protruding eyes

Size: 10–16cm
Habitat: Clear, well-oxygenated mountain streams in deciduous forests extending inland from the Atlantic Iberian coast, with dense surrounding vegetation; up to 1,300m
Reproductive Period: Usually in autumn, with variable short windows depending on local conditions
Sexual Dimorphism: Males are smaller than females, with nuptial pads under their forelimbs and a swollen cloaca
Spawn: Eggs whitish yellow, 3–7mm in diameter; produced in clutches of 10–20; deposited close to stream banks, usually underwater on rocks, roots and aquatic vegetation, or even above water in splash zones; eggs are laid singly, but often found in large assemblages as several females usually spawn in the same place
Larvae: Usually up to 6–7cm; becoming darker with age; very slender, with short gills; short upper tail fin reaching the back; tail tip rounded
Subspecies: Two (page 209)
IUCN Red List: Vulnerable

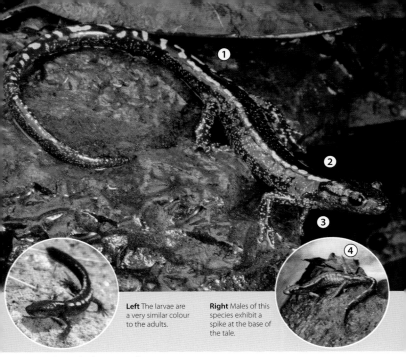

Left The larvae are a very similar colour to the adults.

Right Males of this species exhibit a spike at the base of the tale.

Caucasian Salamanders – *Mertensiella caucasica* sensu lato

This species actually represents two taxa that diverged several millions years ago: *Mertensiella caucasica* sensu stricto, restricted to the Borjomi Gorge in central Georgia (orange star on the map); and a new, yet to be described, taxon, distributed over the rest of the range in the Black Sea basin (orange on the map). Morphological and colour variations cannot be used to separate these two cryptic species. In Caucasian Salamanders, the male has a spike projecting on the upper side of the tail, with which it stimulates the female by opening her cloaca during ventral amplexus. This feature is also present in *Lyciasalamandra*, and for a long time the two were erroneously regarded as close relatives.

Identification Criteria
① Slender body with a long tail
② Dorsal rows of yellow spots
③ Whitish speckles on throat and sides
④ Horn-like protuberance on the dorsal tail surface in males

Size: 13–20cm
Habitat: Streamside habitats in forests with dense vegetation cover; usually narrow, shallow streams; up to 2,800m
Reproductive Period: April–July
Sexual Dimorphism: Males are slightly larger than females and have tail protuberances
Spawn/Larvae: As for Golden-striped Salamander (page 166)
IUCN Red List: Vulnerable (will need reassessment after taxonomic revisions)

Left The species can be identified by its four toes and the V-shaped patch on the head.

Right Spectacled salamanders lay eggs in small clumps in the water.

Northern Spectacled Salamander – *Salamandrina perspicillata*

This tiny salamander is restricted to the north-facing slopes of remote mountain valleys on the western side of the Apennines. During both winter and summer, it hides in rodent burrows or simply underground in the forest, sometimes more than a metre below the surface. Spectacled salamanders display a defensive posture in which they show off their coloured underparts to impress predators and warn them about their toxicity. They may also play dead. Courtship involves a 'waltz', whereby the female follows the male as he dances in circles. The spermatophore is transmitted without amplexus. The shared common name of the spectacled salamanders comes from the V-shaped patches between their eyes, which resemble spectacles.

Identification Criteria
1. Small, slender salamander
2. Dark dorsal coloration, and bright red and white underparts
3. V-shaped whitish-yellow spot between the eyes
4. Four toes only (five in all other salamandrids)
5. Rough, dry skin, covered with tiny warts

Size: 7–12cm

Habitat: Fresh, clear mountain streams in deciduous forests with luxurious vegetation; typically found at 200–900m

Reproductive Period: Usually March–April, but the breeding window can be as long as December–August depending on altitude and conditions

Sexual Dimorphism: Not pronounced; males are slightly smaller, with a higher tail length to body length ratio, and have a slightly bigger cloaca with a longer opening slit

Spawn: Eggs small (5mm with capsule); produced in clutches of 30–60; attached singly or in small clumps to underwater rocks, roots and aquatic vegetation

Larvae: Small, slender larvae (up to 4cm long) with short gills and only four toes; yellow-brown coloration; upper tail fin reaching the middle of the body; tail tip rounded, with a terminal spike

IUCN Red List: Least Concern

Right *Salamandrina* larvae have a large head with short gills and display a brownish coloration.

Southern Spectacled Salamander – *Salamandrina terdigitata*

The Southern Spectacled Salamander is widespread in the Apennines and other mountainous areas in southern Italy. It differs from the Northern Spectacled Salamander (page 168) in its significant genetic divergence and several morphological features. The two species form a narrow hybridisation zone along the Volturno River in south-central Italy. The ecology and reproductive biology of the species are poorly known, but are probably similar to those of its northern counterpart.

Identification Criteria
Similar to Northern Spectacled Salamander but:
① Smaller in size
② More extended red coloration on the tail, reaching the dorsal surface

Size: 5–9cm
Habitat: Shady hillsides in humid valleys with dense vegetation and clear, fresh streams; up to 1,500m
Reproductive Period: April– June
Sexual Dimorphism: As for Northern Spectacled Salamander
Spawn/Larvae: As for Northern Spectacled Salamander
IUCN Red List: Least Concern

Left These colourful species inhabit dry hills in south-western Turkey.

Above and left Lycian salamanders mate in ventral amplexus (above). They can be found hidden between loose rocks and ruins in karstic outcrops (left).

Salamandridae 6 – Lycian Salamanders

The last genus of true salamanders, *Lyciasalamandra*, are spectacularly coloured species native to the south-western Anatolian coast (Lycia) and eastern Aegean islands. As in *Mertensiella*, males have a dorsal tail projection. *Lyciasalamandra* was for long represented by a single species (*L. luschani*), but up to seven species with multiple subspecies are now recognised. According to analyses of molecular evolution, all seem to have arisen simultaneously 10 million years ago, most likely following tectonic events associated with the emergence of the mid-Aegean trench.

All species inhabit Mediterranean shrubland and rocky areas, more specifically (in most species) boulder fields at the foot of karstic limestone formations. Like some drought-adapted *Salamandra* species, Lycian salamanders are viviparous, giving birth to fully formed young. Mating is terrestrial, involving a ventral amplexus, during which the male dorsal projection penetrates the female's cloaca and the spermatophore is released on the ground. All species have a highly restricted distribution and are consequently under direct threat of extinction. Their distribution is the best identification criterion, together with coloration patterns.

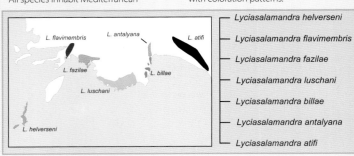

- *Lyciasalamandra helverseni*
- *Lyciasalamandra flavimembris*
- *Lyciasalamandra fazilae*
- *Lyciasalamandra luschani*
- *Lyciasalamandra billae*
- *Lyciasalamandra antalayana*
- *Lyciasalamandra atifi*

L. flavimembris
L. antalyana
L. atifi
L. fazilae
L. billae
L. luschani
L. helverseni

Left This colourful species displays a brown coloration and has yellowish flanks.

Karpathos Lycian Salamander – *Lyciasalamandra helverseni*

Found on the Greek islands of Saria and Kassos, as well as the adjacent island after which it was named, the Karpathos Lycian Salamander is, on average, slightly larger than other members of the genus. It spends much of its life hiding in cool, humid cavities under stones and in cracks in rocks. Mostly nocturnal, the species may also be observed during the day when it rains. When threatened, Lycian salamanders stand on their forelimbs and emit distress calls. They can lose their tail in order to escape predators. This species can be divided into at least two evolutionary lineages which diverged several million years ago.

Identification Criteria
① Medium-sized salamander with large, protruding eyes
② Narrow, elongated parotoid glands
③ Prominent dorsal tail projection in males
④ Translucent belly
⑤ Dark brown coloration with few yellow dots
⑥ Flanks yellowish

Size: 11–15cm
Habitat: Pine forests and maquis shrubland; up to 1,000m
Reproductive Period: Cool winter months; breeds in November–December
Sexual Dimorphism: Males have a dorsal tail projection (up to 5mm), nuptial pads on the forelimbs during the breeding period, and a swollen cloaca (flattened in females)
Spawn/Larvae: Viviparous; females usually give birth to two fully formed young after one year of gestation
IUCN Red List: Vulnerable

Left Subspecies *L. f. ilgazi* has purple coloration with fewer yellowish dots.

Right The typical habitat of this species includes rocky terrain in hilly areas.

Marmaris Lycian Salamander – *Lyciasalamandra flavimembris*

Although distributed over a relatively uninhabited region along the south-western Anatolian coast, from Marmaris to Ula, this Lycian salamander is endangered due to forest fires and overcollection for the pet trade. A different form (*Lyciasalamandra flavimembris ilgazi*) has been described in the area of Muğla, based on morphometric and coloration patterns. New localities are discovered as fieldwork is carried out by herpetologists, and distribution of these subspecies might be broader than previously imagined.

Identification Criteria
Morphologically similar to Karpathos Lycian Salamander (page 171) but:
(1) Shiny, dark brown coloration with yellow/silvery spots, notably on the parotoid glands
(2) Limbs yellowish, tail colour lighter than the back
(3) Gland opening on parotoids visible as dark spots
(4) White iridescent stripe on flank, belly translucent

Size: 11–15cm
Habitat: Pine forests and maquis shrubland on rocky limestone outcrops; up to 600m
Reproductive Period: Cool winter months; breeds November–December
Sexual Dimorphism: As for Karpathos Lycian Salamander
Spawn/Larvae: Viviparous; females usually give birth to one to two fully formed young after one year of gestation
Subspecies: Two (page 209)
IUCN Red List: Endangered

Right This species is mainly red/brown on the back, and white on the flanks and belly.

Fazil Lycian Salamander – *Lyciasalamandra fazilae*

Very common within a restricted range, this species has striking, bright red coloration, which intensifies with age. It is found from Fethiye to Lake Köyceğiz, as well as the coastal islands of Tersane and Domuz. Its ecology and habitat are similar to those for other Lycian salamanders. Versatile predators, Fazil Lycian Salamanders prey on larvae, adult beetles and centipedes.

Identification Criteria
Morphologically similar to Karpathos Lycian Salamander (page 171) but:
① Reddish background coloration with variable amounts of dark blotches
② Flanks whitish and belly pale

Size: 11–15cm
Habitat: Pine forests and maquis shrubland on rocky limestone outcrops; up to 1,000m
Reproductive Period: Cool winter months; breeds November–December
Sexual Dimorphism: As for Karpathos Lycian Salamander
Spawn/Larvae: As for Karpathos Lycian Salamander
IUCN Red List: Endangered

Left The nominal subspecies *L. l. luschani* has a reddish-brown coloration.

Right Subspecies *L. l. finikensis* is darker than the other subspecies.

Luschan's Salamander – *Lyciasalamandra luschani*

The first Lycian salamander to be described, this polytypic taxon was named after Austrian explorer Felix von Luschan (1854–1924). It is a fairly abundant species, displaying strong colour polymorphism between its geographically isolated subspecies. *Lyciasalamandra luschani basoglui* is endemic to the island of Kastellorizo and nearby coast, while *L. l. finikensis* is restricted to the east around the ancient Greek city of Finike. The conservation status of this species should stay stable as long as tourism remains underdeveloped in the region.

Identification Criteria
Morphologically similar to Karpathos Lycian Salamander (page 171) but:
① Dorsal base coloration varies from yellow/red (*L. l. luschani* and *L. l. basoglui*) to brown (*L. l. finikensis*), with differing amounts of dark blotches
② Translucent (*L. l. luschani* and *L. l. basoglui*) or pale (*L. l. finikensis*) venter

Size: 11–15cm
Habitat: Pine forests and maquis shrubland on rocky limestone outcrops; up to 400m
Reproductive Period: Cool winter months; breeds November–December
Sexual Dimorphism: As for Karpathos Lycian Salamander
Spawn/Larvae: As for Karpathos Lycian Salamander
Subspecies: Three (page 210)
IUCN Red List: Vulnerable

Left The genetically different *L. b. yehudai* looks similar to other subspecies.

Right Subspecies *L. b. irfani* has a darker coloration with many speckles.

Bay Lycian Salamander – *Lyciasalamandra billae*

The Bay Lycian Salamander has a complicated taxonomic history. Originally found southwest of Antalya in 1987, and known only from the east slope of the Sarıçınar Dağları (<100km²), it was consequently listed as Critically Endangered. New isolated populations were recently discovered in the nearby Beydağları Mountain range, but described as separate species based on their coloration patterns (*L. arikani*, *L. irfani* and *L. yehudai*). However, more recent genetic analyses have revealed that these are instead subspecies of *L. billae*, which therefore now includes four subspecies. Coloration is quite variable, even within the nominate *L. b. billae*.

Identification Criteria
Morphologically similar to Karpathos Lycian Salamander (page 171) but:
① Coloration ranges from salmon to black with silver-white spots

Size: 11–15cm
Habitat: Pine forests and maquis shrubland on rocky limestone outcrops; up to 200m
Reproductive Period: Cool winter months; breeds November–December
Sexual Dimorphism: As for Karpathos Lycian Salamander
Spawn/Larvae: As for Karpathos Lycian Salamander
Subspecies: Five (page 211)
IUCN Red List: —

Left Note the black spots and yellow coloration on the parotoid.

Right Northern populations consist of subspecies *L. a. gocmeni.*

Anatolia Lycian Salamander – *Lyciasalamandra antalyana*

A yellowish Lycian salamander, restricted to a few populations in the eastern Taurus Mountains. New sites have recently been discovered during herpetological surveys, but because the species has a very narrow distribution it is categorised on the IUCN Red List as Endangered, even though it is locally abundant. In the south-west of its range, the species forms a narrow contact zone with the Bay Lycian Salamander (page 175), involving some hybridisation. The subspecies *Lyciasalamandra antalyana gocmeni* was recently described based on coloration and genetic distinctiveness; its name is a tribute to Bayram Göçmen, a famous Turkish herpetologist and one of the talented photographers who contributed pictures to this book.

Identification Criteria
Morphologically similar to Karpathos Lycian Salamander (page 171) but:
① Base coloration yellow, especially on the parotoid glands and eyes
② Variable dark blotches on the back that may cover most of the yellow base colour
③ Gland opening on parotoids visible as dark spots

Size: 11–15cm
Habitat: Pine forests and maquis shrubland on rocky limestone outcrops; up to 200m
Reproductive Period: Cool winter months; breeds November–December
Sexual Dimorphism: As for Karpathos Lycian Salamander
Spawn/Larvae: As for Karpathos Lycian Salamander
Subspecies: Two (page 212)
IUCN Red List: Endangered

Right Recently hatched, fully-formed juveniles are already half the size of adults.

Atif's Lycian Salamander – *Lyciasalamandra atifi*

Atif's Lycian Salamander is the easternmost member of the genus and also the largest on average. The individuals of some populations are, however, smaller and have been described as different subspecies based on subtle colour differences. Other subspecies have also been described – there are now six in total – however, their validity is pending confirmation from genetic data. The species is highly threatened due to its narrow range and the very few numbers of known populations.

Identification Criteria
Morphologically similar to Karpathos Lycian Salamander (page 171) but:
1. Larger size
2. Brown/greyish coloration with variable amounts of tiny white spots
3. Lateral band consisting of white spots
4. Yellow-red belly

Size: 10–18cm
Habitat: Humid pine forests on rocky limestone outcrops; up to 1,500m
Reproductive Period: Cool winter months; breeds November–December
Sexual Dimorphism: As for Karpathos Lycian Salamander
Spawn/Larvae: As for Karpathos Lycian Salamander
Subspecies: Six (page 212)
IUCN Red List: Endangered

Plethodontidae – Lungless Salamanders

This family is by far the largest in Caudata, with about 380 species. Originally native to the Americas, the lungless salamanders crossed the Bering Strait during the Late Cretaceous and a few relict species remain in Europe today. As their name suggests, these salamanders lack lungs and breathe only through their skin and buccal tissues. Another main character is the presence, in males, of slits (cirri) running along their nasolabial grooves, ending in two small protuberances on the upper lip. These host glands that enhance chemoreception.

The Western Palearctic plethodontids are known as European cave salamanders, and are represented by the endemic genus *Speleomantes* (including eight localised species from mainland Italy and Sardinia). Despite their name, these salamanders are not restricted to caves but also inhabit ground with leaf litter, usually near streams in forest valleys. They are quite agile and can climb vertical cave walls and rocks, thanks to their strong limbs and tail.

Largely nocturnal and completely terrestrial, cave salamanders mate on land during an elaborate courtship display, in which the male waves his tail, rubs the female with his chin (where secretive glands are located), grasps her back and releases a spermatophore, which she then picks up with her cloaca. The female lays up to a dozen eggs in humid spots between rocks in terrestrial habitats. She guards the clutch until the eggs hatch, six to nine months later, and further protects the juveniles for some time after. All species have quite variable coloration; their distribution remains the best identification criterion.

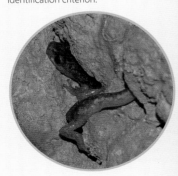

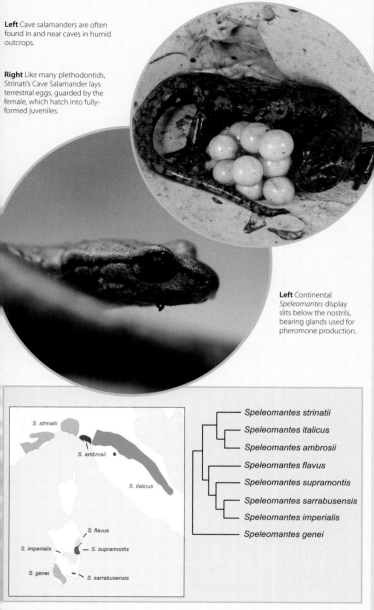

Left Cave salamanders are often found in and near caves in humid outcrops.

Right Like many plethodontids, Strinati's Cave Salamander lays terrestrial eggs, guarded by the female, which hatch into fully-formed juveniles.

Left Continental *Speleomantes* display slits below the nostrils, bearing glands used for pheromone production.

S. strinatii

S. ambrosii

S. italicus

S. flavus

S. imperialis — *S. supramontis*

S. genei — *S. sarrabusensis*

Speleomantes strinatii

Speleomantes italicus

Speleomantes ambrosii

Speleomantes flavus

Speleomantes supramontis

Speleomantes sarrabusensis

Speleomantes imperialis

Speleomantes genei

Left Lungless salamanders are incredibly agile and can often climb cave walls and rocks, as seen here with this Supramonte Cave Salamander.

Left This rock climber features nasolabial slits that are used for chemoreception.

Italian Cave Salamander – *Speleomantes italicus*

A widespread species, the Italian Cave Salamander is found on rocky outcrops in wooded valleys in the northern Apennines. Like other cave salamanders, it has a long, extensible, sticky tongue, which it uses to catch invertebrates. Females protect their eggs against predators and cannibalism, and their secretions prevent fungal infections. Individuals are usually a dark brownish red but can be quite variable in colour, especially in northern ranges, when they sometimes hybridise with Ambrosi's Cave Salamander (page 181). The species is often found in limestone areas, but not exclusively so.

Identification Criteria
1. Stocky salamander with an oval head bearing protruding eyes, a rounded snout and fine parotoid glands
2. Nasolabial slits (cirri) and upper lip glands in males
3. Stubby, flattened toes with partial interdigital webbing
4. Variable grey, brown, greenish or yellowish coloration with spots, stripes, speckles and marbling

Size: Up to 12cm
Habitat: Shaded woodlands in humid stream valleys, with cavities, caves, and rich undergrowth and shelters; up to 1,600m
Reproductive Period: In cool months during winter and spring
Sexual Dimorphism: Males have conspicuous cirri, a pronounced upper-jaw overbite, a glandular swelling on the chin and a swollen cloaca
Spawn/Larvae: Eggs ivory white, large (6mm in diameter); laid in clutches of 5–15 in humid places and guarded by the female
IUCN Red List: Near Threatened

Right The subspecies *S. a. bianchii* (seen here) may in fact belong to the Italian Cave Salamander.

Ambrosi's Cave Salamander – *Speleomantes ambrosii*

Restricted to scattered localities in north-western Italy, this species is nevertheless stable and not under direct threat of extinction. The isolated population in the area of Siena in Tuscany was introduced. The subspecies *Speleomantes ambrosii bianchii* occurs east of the Ligurian Magra River; its status may be challenged as genetic data have shown it to be related to the Italian Cave Salamander (page 180), although it appears unique and different from both that species and *S. a. ambrosii*. The ecology of Ambrosi's Cave Salamander is similar to that of other cave salamanders and its colour patterns are highly variable.

Identification Criteria
Morphologically identical to Italian Cave Salamander and distinguishable only by distribution (see map)

Size: Up to 12cm
Habitat: As for Italian Cave Salamander; up to 1,700m
Reproductive Period: In cool months during winter and spring
Sexual Dimorphism: As for Italian Cave Salamander
Spawn/Larvae: As for Italian Cave Salamander
Subspecies: Two (page 213)
IUCN Red List: Near Threatened

Left This brownish salamander cannot be confused with other amphibians sharing its range.

Right Juveniles are fully formed, like the adults in miniature.

Strinati's Cave Salamander – *Speleomantes strinatii*

Formerly considered a subspecies of the Italian Cave Salamander (page 180) and then Ambrosi's Cave Salamander (page 181), this taxon is restricted to the slopes of the south-eastern coastal French/Italian Alps, as well as the Ligurian Apennines. One population in the Pyrenees originates from an introduction of hybrid specimens in the 1970s from a research station. In its natural range the species is found in scattered localities, where it is locally abundant. Like most members of the genus, Strinati's Cave Salamander is an opportunistic hunter that preys on any invertebrates it can find, notably grasshoppers, beetles and worms.

Identification Criteria
Morphologically identical to Italian Cave Salamander and distinguishable only by distribution (see map)

Size: Up to 12cm
Habitat: As for Italian Cave Salamander; up to 2,300m
Reproductive Period: In cool months during winter and spring
Sexual Dimorphism: As for Italian Cave Salamander
Spawn/Larvae: As for Italian Cave Salamander
IUCN Red List: Near Threatened

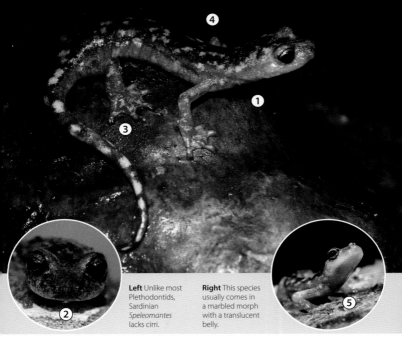

Left Unlike most Plethodontids, Sardinian *Speleomantes* lacks cirri.

Right This species usually comes in a marbled morph with a translucent belly.

Monte Albo Cave Salamander – *Speleomantes flavus*

The largest member of the genus, the Monte Albo Cave Salamander is endemic to the eponymous mountain chain in north-eastern Sardinia, between Siniscola and the Posada River. It usually has yellow-green marbling, but coloration can vary quite significantly between individuals. Although the species is fairly abundant and continuously distributed, its habitat has been deforested for more than a century, and the maquis and primary oak forests it requires are being replaced by dry rocky fields.

Identification Criteria
1. Large size
2. Lacks nasolabial slits (cirri)
3. Toes short and thick, with partial interdigital webbing
4. Individuals generally have yellow-green marbling
5. Belly immaculate and slightly translucent

Size: Up to 15cm
Habitat: Humid mountain areas, with rocky outcrops, cavities and caves, as well as forest areas near brooks; up to 1,000m
Reproductive Period: In cool months during winter and spring
Sexual Dimorphism: Males have a pronounced upper-jaw overbite, a glandular swelling on the chin and a swollen cloaca
Spawn/Larvae: As for Italian Cave Salamander (page 180)
IUCN Red List: Vulnerable

Left The tail acts as a fifth limb, enabling this species to climb rocks.

Right The typical habitat of this species is caves surrounded by mossy boulders.

Supramonte Cave Salamander – *Speleomantes supramontis*

A Sardinian endemic, the Supramonte Cave Salamander is found in the hilly forests of the Supramonte range around the Gulf of Orosei, Nuoro province. It lacks conspicuous cirri and is usually brownish in colour, with dark to greenish marbling. Formerly common and abundant in its natural habitat, it is currently declining and is becoming rarer, most likely due to habitat loss.

Identification Criteria
1. Small cave salamander lacking nasolabial slits (cirri)
2. Dark pigmentation on the belly
3. Usually brown in colour with extensive marbling

Size: Up to 13cm
Habitat: As for Monte Albo Cave Salamander; mostly found on karstic hills with abundant mossy rocks; up to 1,400m
Reproductive Period: In cool months during winter and spring
Sexual Dimorphism: As for Monte Albo Cave Salamander (page 183)
Spawn/Larvae: As for Italian Cave Salamander (page 180)
IUCN Red List: Endangered

Right and far right
This species is highly variable in coloration.

Imperial Cave Salamander – *Speleomantes imperialis*

Sparsely distributed in central and eastern Sardinia, from the coast to Lago Omodeo and Giara di Gesturi, this species has the peculiar habit of releasing an odour along with an urticant liquid when disturbed. The Italians call it *Geotritone Odaroso*, meaning 'sweet-smelling cave salamander'. The species' base colour can be rather bright (type *imperialis*) or darker (type *funereus*). It is the most abundant *Speleomantes* species, with very high local concentrations: hundreds of individuals can be found in the first few metres of a cave near Samugheo, the Grotta degli Spelerpes, which literally means 'cave of the cave salamanders'.

Identification Criteria
① Medium-sized cave salamander lacking nasolabial slits (cirri)
② Short, thick toes with partial interdigital webbing
③ Belly bright and slightly translucent
④ Back purple brownish in colour, with more or less extensive blotched, spotted or marbled patterns

Size: Up to 14cm
Habitat: Humid rocky outcrops with cavities and caves, in forested areas near streams; up to 1,200m
Reproductive Period: In cool months during winter and spring
Sexual Dimorphism: As for Monte Albo Cave Salamander (page 183)
Spawn/Larvae: As for Italian Cave Salamander (page 180)
IUCN Red List: Near Threatened

Left The marbling helps camouflage this salamander against the colourful minerals of cave rocks.

Sette Fratelli Cave Salamander – *Speleomantes sarrabusensis*

Formerly considered a subspecies of the Imperial Cave Salamander (page 185), this taxon is smaller, does not release an odour and its marbling is usually limited to fine spots on the back. It was discovered recently (2001) in a tiny region in the extreme south-east of Sardinia (Sarrabus-Gerrei). No eggs have yet been found for the species, suggesting it might reproduce by viviparity. Its distribution area is dry, consisting of granitic outcrops with Mediterranean vegetation and with few humid caves, potentially limiting the possibilities for egg development. Studies have shown that this species grows up very fast during the first two years of its life, compared to other plethodontids.

Identification Criteria
Similar to Imperial Cave Salamander but:
① Back brownish with lichen-like yellow-green spots

Size: Up to 12cm
Habitat: Forested areas containing granitic rocky outcrops with crevices; up to 900m
Reproductive Period: In cool months during winter and spring
Sexual Dimorphism: As for Imperial Cave Salamander
Spawn/Larvae: Eggs have never been observed; potentially viviparous
IUCN Red List: Vulnerable

Left Unlike other Sardinian cave salamanders, this species has discreet cirri.

Right This brownish species is also called the Brown Cave Salamander.

Gene's Cave Salamander – *Speleomantes genei*

The smallest and darkest member of the European *Speleomantes* genus, Gene's Cave Salamander (often placed in a genus of its own, *Atylodes*, though this is not universally accepted) is endemic to the karstic hills of south-western Sardinia, usually at low elevations (around 300m). Northern and southern populations are genetically divergent and might be candidates for specific taxonomic status. Although there is some variation among individuals, the salamander is dark in colour, often without blotches or marbled patterns. With its habitats subject to deforestation, the species is considered threatened even though it remains common.

Identification Criteria
1. Small cave salamander, occasionally with slightly visible nasolabial slits (cirri)
2. Greyish brown in colour, with very fine golden speckling
3. Belly whitish, often slightly pigmented

Size: Up to 11cm
Habitat: Humid forests in karstic formations with subterranean limestone caverns and rocky ravines, and along brooks; up to 650m
Reproductive Period: In cool months during winter and spring
Sexual Dimorphism: As for Monte Albo Cave Salamander (page 183)
Spawn/Larvae: As for Italian Cave Salamander (page 180)
IUCN Red List: Vulnerable

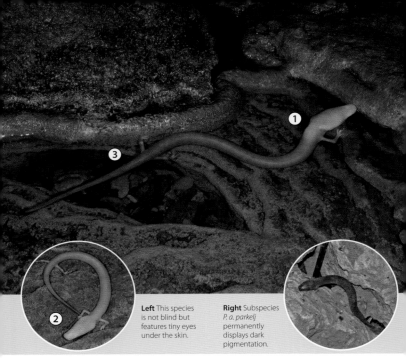

Left This species is not blind but features tiny eyes under the skin.

Right Subspecies *P. a. parkelj* permanently displays dark pigmentation.

OTHER CAUDATA Olm – *Proteus anguinus* (Proteidae)

The Olm is the sole European member of the small North American Proteidae family of completely aquatic neotenous amphibians. Living exclusively in subterranean fresh waters, it is blind and instead uses highly developed olfactory and stream-sensitive senses for foraging and navigation. It can produce melanin when exposed to light, and is therefore not a true albino. Preying on crustaceans, the Olm can survive for up to a decade without food, and its lifespan extends to over a century. Males are territorial, and mating involves pheromone fanning by the male, mate intertwining and external spermatophore transfer. The species is threatened by water pollution.

Identification Criteria
1. Long, slender white/ translucent salamander, with pink gills
2. Minuscule subcutaneous eyes in adults
3. Short limbs with three toes and two fingers

Size: Up to 30cm
Habitat: Cool (5–15°C), well-oxygenated underground water systems; observed in karstic limestone caves; to depths of 300m underground
Reproductive Period: August–April
Sexual Dimorphism: Males have a larger cloaca than females
Spawn: Eggs white, large (8–12mm with capsule); up to 70 deposited under or between rocks in October–March; females guard their clutch for months; occasional viviparity observed: females do not lay eggs but give birth to two fully formed juveniles about 10cm long
Larvae: Small, rudimentary version of adults (2cm long at hatching), with a tail fin, three hind toes and one or two foretoes; upper tail fin extends over most of the back; slight pigmentation in young individuals; viviparous-born juveniles have prominent eyes, which are reabsorbed shortly after birth
IUCN Red List: Vulnerable

Right Note this species only has four toes (compared with five in most salamandrids).

Siberian Newt – *Salamandrella keyserlingii* (Hynobiidae)

With a range of about 12 million km², the Siberian Newt is the most widely distributed amphibian on Earth. It reaches the Western Palearctic in Siberian Russia, where it has colonised a huge variety of biotopes. Siberian Newts overwinter deep in the permafrost or in dead tree trunks. Adapted to exceptional cold, they can survive deep freeze (-45°C), sometimes remaining frozen alive for years. Spawn can also sustain short-term freezing; larvae develop in a few weeks and never overwinter. In members of the family Hynobiidae, fertilisation is mainly external: females lay clutches, which are fertilised by multiple sperm bags from the male (not a single spermatophore) during courtship.

Identification Criteria
1. Small salamander with a rounded head and prominent eyes
2. Bronze-golden coloration, with a silver dorsal band running along the back
3. Well-developed costal grooves and parotoid glands
4. Four toes (five in salamandrids except the Italian endemic *Salamandrina*)

Size: 9–13cm

Habitat: Wet taiga forests and riparian groves in tundra and forest steppes with stagnant and flowing water, such as swamps, lakes and rivers; breeds in all kinds of shallow water bodies with abundant vegetation

Reproductive Period: April–July; breeds after snowmelt

Sexual Dimorphism: Breeding males have a swollen cloaca and a larger tail than females

Spawn: Pairs of elongated egg sacs (connected by a gelatinous filament), each containing about 50–80 light brown eggs, are attached to aquatic vegetation

Larvae: Small (up to 5cm); short, feathery gills; high but short upper tail fin, reaching the tail base; round, light spots on the body and tail fin; four toes only

IUCN Red List: Least Concern

Left The grey coloration and tapered head are typical of this species.

Right This species was originally described from its larvae.

Persian Brook Salamander – *Paradactylodon persicus* (Hynobiidae)

Endemic to the Hyrcanian forests in the mountains facing the Caspian Sea in northern Iran (Ardabil, Gilan, Mazandaran and Golestān provinces), the Persian Brook Salamander was originally described only from its larvae. These can feed in currents using claws to hold onto aquatic vegetation. The life history and ecology of this large salamander are poorly known. It has been recorded preying on bats. While the Persian Brook Salamander is thought to be restricted to caves, it may instead be essentially nocturnal and have a cryptic lifestyle. So far, the species is known from only few scattered localities. Some authors consider the Shirabad cave population to be a different taxon (orange star on the map).

Identification Criteria

1. Large salamander with a flattened head and protruding eyes
2. Shiny, deep violet or grey base colour with yellow markings
3. 11–14 costal grooves clearly visible
4. Four toes and fingers

Size: Usually 20–23cm and up to 27cm (few specimen have been studied)

Habitat: Fast-flowing montane streams in the Caspian Hyrcanian mixed forests and nearby caves

Reproductive Period: Not documented; probably during the first part of the year, in January–May

Sexual Dimorphism: Not studied; as in other Caudata, males must have a swollen cloaca

Spawn: Produces pairs of egg sacs containing 30–50 yellowish eggs, which are attached to stones

Larvae: Most likely overwinter, growing up to 10cm; light yellow coloration, gaining dark grey spots with age; large head with large gills; four digits on each limb, ending in black horny pads; large upper tail fin reaching the base of the head

IUCN Red List: Near Threatened

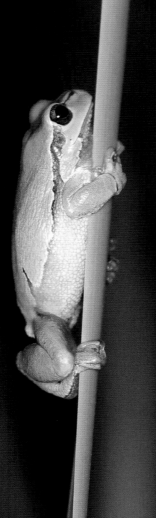

SUBSPECIES APPENDIX

Common Midwife Toad – *Alytes obstetricans*

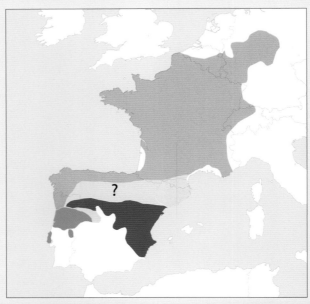

A. o. obstetricans

A. o. almogavarii

A. o. pertinax

A. o. boscai

Painted Frog – *Discoglossus pictus*

D. p. pictus

D. p. auritus

Yellow-bellied Toad – *Bombina variegata*

 B. v. variegata

B. v. scabra

European Green Toad – *Bufotes viridis*

B. v. viridis

B. v. variabilis

 Hybrids or both

Common Frog – *Rana temporaria*

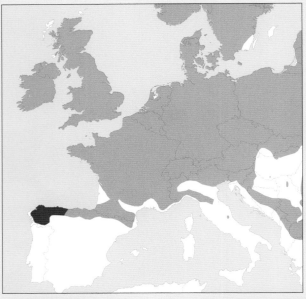

R. t. temporaria

R. t. parvipalmata, generally smaller and reduced feet webbing; probably represents a distinct species

Moor Frog – *Rana arvalis*

R. a. arvalis

R. a. wolterstorfii

Sahara Frog – *Pelophylax saharicus*

P. s. saharicus

P. s. riodeoroi

Smooth Newt – *Lissotriton vulgaris*

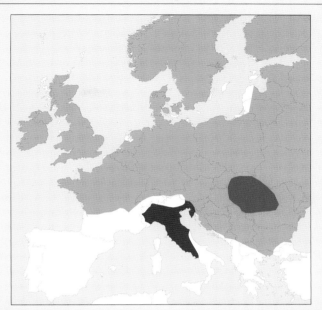

L. v. vulgaris, ragged crest morphotype

L. v. meridionalis, smooth crest morphotype

L. v. ampelensis, smooth crest morphotype

Bosca's Newt – *Lissotriton boscai*

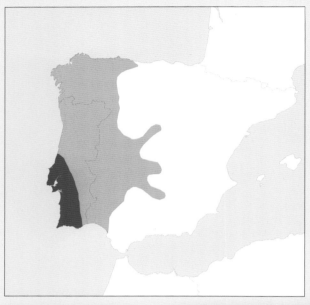

L. b. boscai, large size (7–10cm)

L. b. maltzani, small size (5–8cm), more colourful back

Alpine Newt – *Ichthyosaura alpestris*

I. a. alpestris, Carpathians and Balkan populations form distinct lineages

I. a. cyreni

I. a. apuana (north-western Italy)

I. a. inexpectata (southern Italy)

I. a. montenegrina, including former
subspecies *I. a. reiseri*, *I. a. serdara*,
I. a. piperiana

I. a. veluchiensis

★ undescribed taxon from Vlasina lake, Serbia

Southern Banded Newt – *Ommatotriton vittatus*

O. v. vittatus

O. v. cilicensis, eastern distribution
unclear

Strauch's Spotted Newt – *Neurergus strauchii*

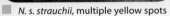 *N. s. strauchii,* multiple yellow spots   ■ *N. s. barani,* scattered yellow spots

★ *N. s. munzurensis,* tiny yellow speckles – validity unclear

Common Fire Salamander – *Salamandra salamandra*

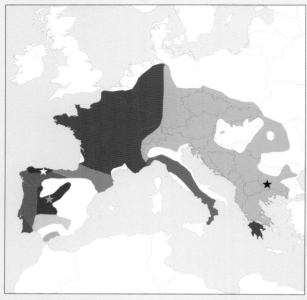

S. s. *salamandra*, irregular yellow spots

S. s. *terrestris*, yellow spots arranged in two dorsal lines

S. s. *fastuosa*, truncated snout, two yellow dorsal bands of varying width; frequently viviparous

S. s. *bernardezi*, two yellow dorsal bands with varying amounts of black; frequently viviparous

☆ *S. s. alfredschmidti,* small (10cm), almost entirely yellow with black/ brownish speckles; Rio Tendi and Marea valleys; frequently viviparous

■ *S. s. gallaica,* pointy snout, large yellow spots, sometimes reddish, can grow big (>30cm)

■ *S. s. crespoi,* pointy snout, small yellow spots, sometimes reddish

■ *S. s. bejarae,* irregular spots, up to 2,500m

★ *S. s. almanzoris,* small, high-altitude subspecies (around 2,000m) from the Sierra de Gredos; tail compressed, sometimes almost entirely black

□ *S. s. morenica,* yellow and red dots (especially on the head); found around 1,000m

■ *S. s. longirostris,* very pointed snout, sometimes considered as a valid species

■ *S. s. gigliolii,* large and flat head, extensive yellow spots

★ *S. s. beschkovi*, short limbs, variable yellow spots; Sandanski-Bistrica valley in Pirim Mountains, Bulgaria

▇ *S. s. werneri*, morphologically similar to *S. s. salamandra*; Pelion, Euboa, Kyllini and Taygetos Mountains, southern Greece

North African Fire Salamander – *Salamandra algira*

▇ *S. a. algira*

▇ *S. a. tingitana*, no red patches, but whitish speckles on the ventral side

▇ *S. a. splendens*, red patches present, sometimes dominating the yellow

★ *S. a. spelaea*, large yellow patches and few red marks; restricted to Beni Snassen massif in NE Morocco, and perhaps Rarh el Maden in SW Algeria

Near Eastern Fire Salamander –
Salamandra infraimmaculata

S. i. infraimmaculata, mostly large yellow patches

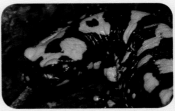

S. i. orientalis, presence of small yellow spots

S. i. semenovi, rounded yellow spots

Alpine Salamander – *Salamandra atra*

▢ *S. a. atra*, fully black

☆ *S. a. pasubiensis*, a few tiny yellow spots, usually at the basis of the legs or head; Pasubio Mountain in the Venetian Alps (1,500–1,800m)

★ *S. a. aurorae*, black with large yellow patches; between Trento and Asiago in the Venetian Alps (1,300–1,800m)

Golden-striped Salamander – *Chioglossa lusitanica*

C. l. longipes, longer limbs and toes than *C. l. lusitanica*

C. l. lusitanica

Marmaris Lycian Salamander – *Lyciasalamandra flavimembris*

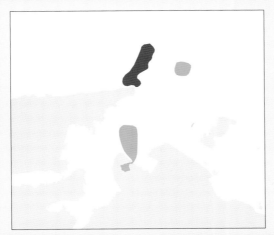

L. f. flavimembris, many yellowish dots; parotoids and hindlimbs yellowish

L. f. ilgazi, few yellowish dots; parotoids and hindlimbs with background purplish coloration

Luschan's Salamander – *Lyciasalamandra luschani*

L. l. luschani, silver colour with extensive dark patches

L. l. basoglui, brownish red coloration

L. l. finikensis, dark with white spots

Bay Lycian Salamander – *Lyciasalamandra billae*

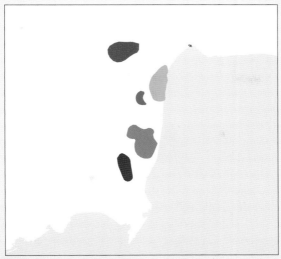

Subdivision into five subspecies (at least four bearing significant genetic divergence), with subtle variation in colour patterns.

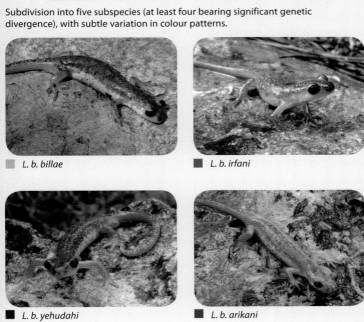

■ *L. b. billae*

■ *L. b. irfani*

■ *L. b. yehudahi*

■ *L. b. arikani*

■ *L. b. eikeae*

Anatolia Lycian Salamander –
Lyciasalamandra antalyana

■ *L. a. antalyana*, yellow coloration limited to the head

■ *L. a. gocmeni*, yellow dorsal and supracaudal markings

Atif's Lycian Salamander – *Lyciasalamandra atifi*

Subdivision into six subspecies with subtle colour and size variation, pending genetic validation.

■ *L. a. atifi*   ■ *L. a. godmanni*

■ *L. a. bayrami*   ■ *L. a. kunti*

■ *L. a. oezi*   ■ *L. a. veithi*

Ambrosi's Cave Salamander –
Speleomantes ambrosii

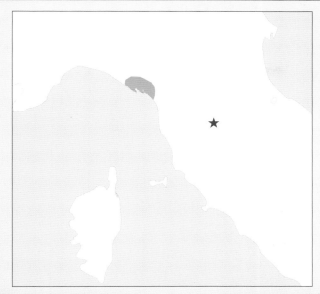

S. a. ambrosii, two diffuse dorsal-lateral bands

★ *S. a. bianchii*, dorso-lateral bands absent

Acknowledgements

This book is the product of a three-year-long journey that I can describe without hesitation as the most collaborative so far in my career as a herpetological researcher. I have drawn on a vast network of wildlife photographers, field herpetologists, terrarium breeders, academic researchers, and enthusiasts who simply enjoy observing the wildlife in their own backyards. Throughout this project, I have also reconnected with former colleagues and old friends, and made many new ones, and some of these encounters have subsequently blossomed into professional collaborations.

Thanks must go to many of these people, without whom this chicken would have probably died in the egg, to quote the French equivalent of 'nipped in the bud'. Citing the first and most important of them brings me back to the very genesis of this book. In the summer of 2015, I was in Finland, catching butterflies for the research project of fellow biologist and wildlife photographer Mila Pajković. We both had little clue about butterflies at first, but became specialists in a matter a weeks thanks to a nicely designed field guide, *Butterflies of Britain and Europe: A Photographic Guide*, by Tari Haahtela and colleagues. And there we were, one evening in Lapland, thinking that such a practical handbook should also exist for my favourite animals, the amphibians. In the following months, Mila played an instrumental role in the birth of this book, its design, content and spirit, which Bloomsbury kindly agreed to support. In addition to my deepest gratitude for her contribution and encouragement, I hope she will be pleased with the result.

My next thoughts go to my PhD advisor, Nicolas Perrin. His dedicated mentorship for more than a decade has shaped the researcher I have become and stimulated my passion for nature. As I am writing these lines from his garden in France, surrounded by the nearby calls of Natterjack Toads, I feel extremely humble to have had his support and friendship, and I am proud that this book bears his foreword (page 6), as well as a species named after him (page 63).

Two key members of the vast network mentioned above are Nicolas Rodrigues, the skilled artist who sketched the original drawings featured in this book's introduction (pages 12–16), and Sylvain Dubey, a first-class herpetologist and long-term collaborator, who contributed many photos and a great deal of advice. Their friendship and enthusiasm are greatly appreciated.

Many research colleagues also came forward when I needed materials and information, among them Spartak Litvinchuk, Inigo Martinez-Solano, Glib Mazepa, Mathieu Denöel, Mario Lo Valvo, Philippe Géniez, Pierre-André Crochet, Miguel Vences, Ilias Strachinis, Nataliia Suriadna, Matthieu Berroneau and Quentin Martinez. I look forward to our future collaborations.

This project also gave me the opportunity to appreciate the work of many talented photographers, both amateur and professional, who kindly agreed to contribute pictures. Philippe Evrard is a naturalist who co-authored the *Guide des amphibiens et reptiles de France* (Belin editions, 2012); many photos, notably those of clutches, larvae and habitats, were taken by him. Laura and Bobby Bok are wildlife photographers and herpetologists who have portrayed several amphibians from the edges of the Western Palearctic; their astonishing work can also be enjoyed in the *Field Guide to the Amphibians and Reptiles of Britain and Europe* (Bloomsbury, 2016). Dennis Hägg is a passionate herpetologist from Sweden, and Sebastian Voitel has travelled the world to appreciate salamander diversity. Both contributed a number of photographs, especially of the Lycian salamanders from south-western Turkey. Alexandre Roux is a wildlife biologist in charge of the herpetologist group in the area of Lyon, and he has spent many nights searching for and photographing species in Western Europe. Some pictures from Iberian and Moroccan species were taken by Alberto Sanchez Vialas, a Spanish herpetologist and wildlife photographer undertaking a PhD in biology. Henk Wallays has an amazing collection of urodeles that he has photographed for this book. Joachim Nerz is a German herpetologist with a broad interest in salamanders, and he has contributed pictures from all over the Western Palearctic. Thanks must also go to the following photographers: Andreas Nöllert, Barbod Safaei Marhoo, Frank Deschandol, Konstantinos Kalaentzis, David Herrero Gonzalez, Fabio Savini, Adem Adakul, Mattjis Hollanders, Claudine Delmas, George Wilkinson, Mario Riedling, Edvard Mizsei, Florian Bégou, Marco Bertolini, Alexandre Ville, Daniel Escoriza, Gabriel Martinez, Marco Maggesi, Alexandar Simovic, Andrew Smith, Bayram Gocmen, Guy Haimovich, Jihène Ben Hassine, Matthew Smith, Cyril Ruoso, Sergio Gutierrez, Marine Pézin, Javier Gallego, Jan Jezek, Ivan Marin, Arnaud Jamin, Vincent Rivère, Jérémy Jalabert, Philip de Pous, Adrien Sprumont, Trevor Willis, David Potter, Georgi Popgeorgiev, Elias Tzoras, Olivier Peyre, Milan Zygmunt, Sergey Uryadnikov and Emil von Maltitz. I am thankful and honoured to be able to include their photos in this book.

The Bloomsbury editorial team and their associates were of course instrumental. I would like to thank Jim Martin (the publisher) for supporting the project, as well as Jenny Campbell (my editor), Rod Teasdale (the designer) and Susi Bailey (the copy-editor), for their day-to-day assistance and feedback, along with their enthusiasm and patience.

Last but not least, I would like to mention the hundreds of animals we spent countless hours searching for and photographing, and, by extension, disturbing. Amphibians are amazing subjects to observe, and I would encourage everyone to go and look for them, but always to remain respectful of them and their threatened environments.

Image Credits

Bloomsbury Publishing would like to thank the following for providing photographs and permission to reproduce copyright material. While every effort has been made to trace and acknowledge all copyright holders, we would like to apologise for any errors or omissions and invite readers to inform us so that corrections can be made in any future editions of the book.

Key t = top; l = left; r = right; tl = top left; tcl = top centre left; tc = top centre; tcr = top centre right; tr = top right; cl = centre left; c = centre; cr = centre right; b = bottom; bl = bottom left; bcl = bottom centre left; bc = bottom centre; bcr = bottom centre right; br = bottom right

tl Christophe Dufresnes, tr Dennis Hägg, cl Philippe Evrard, cr Philippe Evrard, b Mathieu Denoël; **122** t Andreas Nöllert, cl Alexandre Roux, cr Alexandre Roux; **123** t Konstantinos Kalaentzis, cl Konstantinos Kalaentzis; **124** t Pierre-André Crochet, cl Pierre-André Crochet, cr Pierre-André Crochet; **125** t Frank Deschandol (frank-deschandol.com), cr Frank Deschandol (frank-deschandol.com); **126** t Arnaud Jamin, cl Sylvain Dubey; **127** t Henk Wallays (intruigingnature.photodeck.com), cl Sebastian Voitel, cr Sebastian Voitel; **128** t Philippe Evrard, cl Philippe Evrard, cr Philippe Evrard; **129** t Alberto Sanchez Vialas, cl Dennis Hägg, cr Henk Wallays (intruigingnature.photodeck.com); **130** t George Wilkinson, cl Philippe Evrard; **131** t Sylvain Dubey, cl Philippe Evrard, cr Sylvain Dubey; **132** l Gabriel Martinez, tr Philippe Evrard, cr Sylvain Dubey; **133** t Philippe Evrard, cl Philippe Evrard, cr Christophe Dufresnes; **134** t Sebastian Voitel, cl Philippe Evrard, cr Alexandre Roux; **135** t Mario Riedling, cl Joachim Nerz, cr Henk Wallays (intruigingnature.photodeck.com); **136** t Edvard Mizsei, cl Vincent Rivière, cr t Henk Wallays (intruigingnature. photodeck.com), cl Pierre-André Crochet, cr Pierre-André Crochet; **138** t Henk Wallays (intruigingnature.photodeck. com), Ilias Strachinis (herpetofauna.gr); **139** t Adem Adakul, cr Laura Bok; **140** t Philippe Evrard, cl Philippe Evrard, cr Inigo Martinez-Solano; **141** t Christophe Dufresnes, cl Dennis Hägg, cr Mattjis Hollanders; **142** tl Barbod Safaei Marhoo, l George Wilkinson, cr Barbod Safaei Marhoo, bc Sylvain Dubey; **143** t Laura Bok, cl Spartak Litvinchuk, cr Sylvain Dubey; **144** t Spartak Litvinchuk, cl Pierre-André Crochet; **145** t Sebastian Voitel, cl Laura Bok, cr Joachim Nerz; **146** t Laura Bok, cl Barbod Safaei Marhoo, cr Barbod Safaei Marhoo; **147** t Laura Bok, cl Sebastian Voitel, cr Sebastian Voitel; **148** t Henk Wallays (intruigingnature.photodeck.com), cl Barbod Safaei Marhoo; **149** t Laura Bok, cl Barbod Safaei Marhoo, cr Barbod Safaei Marhoo; **150** tc Henk Wallays (intruigingnature.photodeck.com), tr Sebastian Voitel, l Philippe Evrard, bc Christophe Dufresnes; **151** t Alexandre Roux, cl Sebastian Voitel, cr Mattjis Hollanders; **152** t Alberto Sanchez Vialas, cl Alexandre Roux; **153** t Philippe Evrard, cl Jeremy Jalabert, cr Alexandre Roux; **154** t George Wilkinson, cl Dennis Hägg, cr Henk Wallays (intruigingnature.photodeck.com); **155** t Christophe Dufresnes, cl Laura Bok, cr Daniel Escoriza; **156** t Henk Wallays (intruigingnature.photodeck.com), Philip de Pous; **157** t Daniel Escoriza, cr Jalel l'Apiculteur/Wikipedia; **158** David Herrero Gonzalez; **159** tl Alexandre Roux, tr Marco Bertolini, c Joachim Nerz, b Fabio Savini (flickr.com/photos/fabio-savini-naturalistic-photo); **160** t Alexandar Simovic, cl Mattjis Hollanders, cr Alexandre Roux; **161** t Claudine Delmas, cl Philippe Evrard, cr Philippe Evrard; **162** t Laura Bok, cl Alberto Sanchez Vialas, cr Alberto Sanchez Vialas; **163** t Laura & Bobby Bok, cl Guy Haimovich, cr Laura Bok; **164** t Christophe Dufresnes, cl Dennis Hägg, cr Fabio Savini (flickr.com/photos/fabio-savini-naturalistic-photo); **165** t Marco Maggesi, cl Dennis Hägg, cr Sebastian Voitel; **166** t Dennis Hägg, cl Joachim Nerz, cr Dennis Hägg; **167** t Laura Bok, cl Sebastian Voitel, cr Laura & Bobby Bok; **168** t Fabio Savini (flickr.com/photos/fabio-savini-naturalistic-photo), cl Alexandre Roux, cr Philippe Evrard; **169** t Adrien Sprumont, cr De Agostini Picture Library/Contributor/Getty; **170** tc Dennis Hägg, l Sebastian Voitel, cr Konstantinos Kalaentzis, bc Dennis Hägg; **171** t Sebastian Voitel, cl Sebastian Voitel; **172** t Dennis Hägg, cl Dennis Hägg, cr Sebastian Voitel; **173** t Sebastian Voitel, cr Sebastian Voitel; **174** t Sebastian Voitel, cl Sebastian Voitel, cr Dennis Hägg; **175** t Dennis Hägg, cl Dennis Hägg, cr Dennis Hägg; **176** t Sebastian Voitel, cl Dennis Hägg, cr Dennis Hägg; **177** t Sebastian Voitel, cr Dennis Hägg; **178** t Joachim Nerz, b Andreas Nöllert; **179** t Matthieu Berroneau (matthieu-berroneau.fr), cr Fabio Savini (flickr.com/photos/fabio-savini-naturalistic-photo); **180** t Alexandre Roux, cl Fabio Savini (flickr.com/photos/fabio-savini-naturalistic-photo); **181** t Frank Deschandol (frank-deschandol.com), cr Frank Deschandol (frank-deschandol.com); **182** t Dennis Hägg, cl Alexandre Roux, cr Florian Bégou; **183** t Dennis Hägg, cl Mario Riedling, cr Dennis Hägg; **184** t Dennis Hägg, cl Mario Riedling, cr Philippe Evrard; **185** t Joachim Nerz, cl Joachim Nerz, cr Philippe Evrard; **186** t Frank Deschandol (frank-deschandol.com), cl Frank Deschandol (frank-deschandol.com); **187** t Mario Riedling, cl Mario Riedling, cr Joachim Nerz; **188** t Sebastian Voitel, cl Sebastian Voitel, cr Sebastian Voitel; **189** t Henk Wallays (intruigingnature. photodeck.com), cr Pierre-André Crochet; **190** t Laura Bok, cl Laura Bok, cr Barbod Safaei Marhoo; **191** Christophe Dufresnes; **192** cl Christophe Dufresnes, cr Alberto Sanchez Vialas, bl Alberto Sanchez Vialas, br Trevor Willis; **193** cl Laura Bok, cr Inigo Martinez-Solano; **194** cl Christophe Dufresnes, cr Philippe Géniez; **195** cl Dennis Hägg, cr Konstantinos Kalaentzis; **196** cl Christophe Dufresnes, cr Andreas Nöllert; **197** cl Philippe Evrard, cr Andreas Nöllert; **198** cl Jihene Ben Hassine, cr Alexandre Roux; **199** cl David Potter, cr Philippe Evrard, bl blickwinkel/Alamy Stock Photo; **200** cl Alberto Sanchez Vialas, cr Philippe Evrard; **201** cl Christophe Dufresnes, cr Sebastian Voitel, bl Joachim Nerz, br Henk Wallays (intruigingnature.photodeck.com); **202** tl Henk Wallays (intruigingnature.photodeck.com), tr Henk Wallays (intruigingnature.photodeck.com), bl Laura Bok, br Sebastian Voitel; **203** cl Sebastian Voitel, cr Sebastian Voitel; **204** cl Sylvain Dubey, cr Christophe Dufresnes, bl Claudine Delmas, br David Herrero Gonzalez; **205** tl Sebastian Voitel, tr Dennis Hägg, cl1 Dennis Hägg, cr1 David Herrero Gonzalez, cl2 David Herrero Gonzalez, cr2 Andreas Nöllert, bl Alberto Sanchez Vialas, br Joachim Nerz; **206** tl Georgi Popgeorgiev, tr Elias Tzoras, cl Olivier Peyre, cr Joachim Nerz, bl Laura Bok, br Daniel Escoriza; **207** cl Laura & Bobby Bok, cr Henk Wallays (intruigingnature. photodeck.com), bl Laura Bok; **208** cl Christophe Dufresnes, cr Fabio Savini (flickr.com/photos/fabio-savini-naturalistic-photo), bl Fabio Savini (flickr.com/photos/fabio-savini-naturalistic-photo); **209** tr Dennis Hägg, bl Dennis Hägg, br Dennis Hägg; **210** cl Dennis Hägg, cr Dennis Hägg, bl Sebastian Voitel; **211** cl Sebastian Voitel, cr Sebastian Voitel, bl Sebastian Voitel, cr Sebastian Voitel; **212** tc Sebastian Voitel, cr Dennis Hägg; **213** Sebastian Voitel; **214** cl Alexandre Roux, cr Frank Deschandol.

Further Reading and Resources

Books
The following are great sources of general information, and some of their authors (Andreas Nöllert, Bobby Bok, Bayram Göçmen , Phillipe Evrard, Phillipe Géniez) kindly contributed to this book.

Arnold N, Ovenden D. *Reptiles and Amphibians of Britain and Europe.* HarperCollins, London 2002.
Bahaa El Din S. *A Guide to the Reptiles and Amphibians of Egypt.* The American University in Cairo Press, Cairo 2006.
Bar A, Haimovitch G. *A Field Guide to Reptiles and Amphibians of Israel.* Pazbar LTD, Israel 2011.
Budak A, Göçmen B. *Herpetology.* Ege Üniversitesi Fen Fakültesi Kitaplar Serisi, No. 194, Ege Üniversitesi Basimevi, Bornova-Izmir, 2005, 226 pp. In Turkish.
Evrard P, Thirion JM. *Guide des amphibiens et reptiles de France.* Belin, 2012, In French.
Geniez P, Mateo JA, Geniez M, Pether J, Böhme W. *The Amphibians and Reptiles of the Western Sahara: An Atlas and Field Guide.* Chimaira, Frankfurt 2004.
Kwet A. *Guide to the reptiles and amphibians of Europe.* New Holland, London 2009.
Nöllert A, Nöllert C. *Die Amphibien Europas.* Franckh-Kosmos Verlags-GmbH & Co, Stuttgart 2003.
Pysanets Y. *The amphibians of Ukraine.* Rayevsky Scientific Publishers, Kiev 2007. In Ukrainian.
Sparreboom M. *Salamanders of the Old World: the Salamanders of Europe, Asia and Northern Africa.* KNNV Publishing, Leiden 2014.
Speybroeck J, Beukema W, Bok B, Van Der Voort J. *Field Guide to the Amphibians and Reptiles of Britain and Europe.* Bloomsbury Wildlife, London 2016.
Tarkhnishvili DN, Gokhelashvili RK. *The amphibians of the Caucasus.* Pensoft, Sofia-Moscow 1999.

Websites
Online resources with useful information, pictures and herp trip reports:

AmphibiaWeb: amphibiaweb.org
Herpetofauna of Europe: hylawerkgroep.be/jeroen/index. php?id=1
Herping: frank-deschandol.com/rips-herpeto
Moroccoherps: moroccoherps.com/en/Inicio

Scientific Literature
The following lists scientific publications upon which some of the content of this book is based. It is obviously far from exhaustive, but features good starting points for interested readers.

Afroosheh M, et al. *Distribution and abundance of the endangered yellow spotted mountain newt Neurergus microspilotus (Caudata: Salamandridae) in Western Iran.* Herpetological Conservation and Biology 2016; 11: 52–60.
Afsar M, Afsar B, Arikan H. *Classification of the mountain frogs of the Berçelan Plateau (Hakkari), east Anatolia (Turkey) (Anura: Ranidae).* Herpetozoa 2015; 28: 15–27.
Akin C, et al. *Phylogeographic patterns of genetic diversity in eastern Mediterranean water frogs were determined by geological processes and climate change in the Late Cenozoic.* Journal of Biogeography 2010; 37: 2111–2124.
Akman B, Godmann O. *A new subspecies of Lyciasalamandra antalyana (Amphibia: Salamandridae) from the Lycian coast, Turkey.* Salamandra 2014; 50: 125–132.
Alford RA, Richards SJ. *Global amphibian declines: a problem in applied ecology.* Annual Review in Ecology and Systematics 1999; 30: 133–165.
Allentoft ME, O'Brien J. *Global amphibian declines, loss of genetic diversity and fitness: a review.* Diversity 2010; 2: 47–71.
Amor N, et al. *Karyological and morphometric variation of the North African green frog Pelophylax saharicus (Anura) in north-eastern Africa.* Current Zoology 2010; 56: 678–686.
Andreone F, Clima V, de Michelis S. *On the ecology of Salamandra lanzai Nascetti, Andreone, Capula & Bullini, 1988. Number of movement of individuals, and influence of climate on activity in a population of the upper Po Valley (Caudata: Salamandridae).* Herpetozoa 1999; 12: 3–10.
Arikan H, et al. *A taxonomical study on the Rana ridibunda Pallas, 1771 (Anura: Ranidae) population from Ivriz-Eregli (Konya).* Turkish Journal of Zoology 1998; 22: 181–184.
Arikan H, et al. *Some comments on the breeding biology of Pelodytes caucasicus Boulenger, 1896 (Anura: Pelodytidae) from Uzungöl, Northeast Anatolia.* Turkish Journal of Zoology 2007; 31: 53–64.
Arntzen JW, Olgun K. *Taxonomy of the banded newt, Triturus vittatus: morphological and allozyme data.* Amphibia-Reptilia 2000; 21: 155–168.
Arntzen JW, et al. *Geographical variation in the golden striped salamander, Chioglossa lusitanica Bocage, 1864 and the description of a newly recognized subspecies.* Journal of Natural History 2007; 41: 925–936.
Arntzen JW, et al. *Asymmetric viability of reciprocal-cross hybrids between crested and marbled newts (Triturus cristatus and T. marmoratus).* Evolution 2009; 63: 1191–1202.
Arntzen JW, et al. *Morphological and genetic differentiation of Bufo toads: two cryptic species in Western Europe (Anura, Bufonidae).* Contributions to Zoology 2013; 82: 147–169.
Arntzen JW, Wielstra B, Wallis GP. *The modality of nine Triturus newt hybrid zones assessed with nuclear, mitochondrial and morphological data.* Biological Journal of the Linnean Society 2014; 113: 604–622.
Auliya M, et al. *The global amphibian trade flows through Europe: the need for enforcing and improving legislation.* Biodiversity and Conservation 2016; 25: 2581–2595.
Babik W, et al. *Mitochondrial phylogeography of the moor frog, Rana arvalis.* Molecular Ecology 2004; 13: 1469–1480.
Baha El, Din SM. *A new species of toad (Anura: Bufonidae) from Egypt.* The Journal of the Herpetological Association of Africa 1993; 42: 24–27.
Baskale E, Sayim F, Kaya U. *Body size and reproductive characteristics of paedomorphic and metamorphic individuals of the northern banded newt (Ommatotriton ophryticus).* Acta Herpetologica 2011; 6: 19–25.
Beebee TJC. *Conservation genetics of amphibians.* Heredity 2005; 95: 423–427.
Beser N, et al. *Age structure and body size of Mertensiella caucasica (Waga, 1876) (Caudata: Salamandridae) in a population from Turkey.* Russian Journal of Herpetology 2017; 24: 202–208.
Bhandari RK, et al. *Effects of the environmental estrogenic contaminants bisphenol A and 17a-ethinyl estradiol on sexual development and adult behaviors in aquatic wildlife species.* General and Comparative Endocrinology 2015; 214: 195–219.
Bisconti R, et al. *Predation by the Italian pool frog Pelophylax lessonae bergeri on the Valais shrew, Sorex antinorii.* Herpetology Notes 2014; 7: 159–160.
Biton R, et al. *The rediscovered Hula*

painted frog is a living fossil. Nature Communications 2013; 4: 1–6.

Blaustein AR, *et al.* *Direct and indirect effects of climate change on amphibian populations.* Diversity 2010; 2: 281–313.

Bogaerts S, *et al.* *Distribution, ecology and conservation of Ommatotriton vittatus and Salamandra infraimmaculata in Syria.* Salamandra 2013; 49: 87–96.

Boukema W, *et al.* *Review of the systematics, distribution, biogeography and natural history of Moroccan amphibians.* Zootaxa 2013; 3661: 1–60.

Brühl CA, *et al.* *Terrestrial pesticide exposure of amphibians: An underestimated cause of global decline?* Scientific Reports 2013; 3: 1135.

Bucciarelli GM, *et al.* *Invasion complexities: the diverse impacts of non-native species on amphibians.* Copeia 2014; 4: 611–632.

Budak A, Tok CV. *On specimens of Rana ridibunda Pallas, 1771 (Anura: Ranidae) collected from Isikli lake (Civril-Denizli).* Turkish Journal of Zoology 2000; 24: 135–137.

Bülbül U, Kutrup B. *Morphological and genetic variations of Ommatotriton in Turkey.* Animal Biology 2013; 63: 297–312.

Busak SD. *Biochemical and morphological differentiation in Spanish and Moroccan populations of Discoglossus and the description of a new species from southern Spain (Amphibia, Anura, Discoglossidae).* Annals of Carnegie Museum 1986; 55: 41–61.

Canestrelli D, Nascetti G. *Phylogeography of the pool frog Rana (Pelophylax) lessonae in the Italian peninsula and Sicily: multiple refugia, glacial expansions and nuclear-mitochondrial discordance.* Journal of Biogeography 2008; 35: 1923–1936.

Canestrelli D, Sacco F, Nascetti G. *On glacial refugia, genetic diversity, and microevolutionary processes: deep phylogeographical structure in the endemic newt Lissotriton italicus.* Biological Journal of the Linnean Society 2012; 105: 42–55.

Canestrelli D, *et al.* *What triggers the rising of an intraspecific biodiversity hotspot? Hints from the agile frog.* Scientific Reports 2014; 4: 5042.

Carranza S, Amat F. *Taxonomy, biogeography and evolution of Euproctus (Amphibia:Salamandridae), with the resurrection of the genus Calotriton and the description of a new endemic species from the Iberian Peninsula.* Zoological Journal of the Linnean Society 2005; 145: 555–582.

Carey C, Alexander MA. *Climate change and amphibian declines: is*

there a link? Diversity and Distribution 2003; 9: 111–121.

Cevik IE, *et al.* *Comparative morphological and serological studies of three Anatolian mountain frogs, Rana macrocnemis, R. camerani and R. holtzi (Anura, Ranidae).* Amphibia-Reptilia 2006; 27: 63–71.

Chiari Y, *et al.* *Phylogeography of Sardinian cave salamanders (Genus Hydromantes) is mainly determined by geomorphology.* PLoS ONE 2012; 7: e32332.

Chubinishvili AT, Gokhelashvili RK, Tarkhnishvili DN. *Population ecology of the Caucasian Parsley frog (Pelodytes caucasicus Boulenger) in the Borjomi Canyon.* Russian Journal of Herpetology 1995; 2: 79–86.

Cicek K, *et al.* *Food habits of the Lycian salamander, Lyciasalamandra fazilae (Basoglu and Atatür, 1974): Preliminary data on Dalyan population.* North-Western Journal of Zoology 2007; 3: 1–8.

Cicek K, *et al.* *Food composition of Uludag frog, Rana macrocnemis Bouienger, 1885 in Uludag (Bursa, Turkey).* Acta Herpetologica 2011; 6: 87–99.

Cicek K, Ayaz D, Bayrakci Y. *Morphology of the northern banded newt, (Ommatotriton ophryticus) (Berthold, 1846) (Caudata: Salamandridae) in Uludag (Bursa, Turkey).* Herpetology Notes 2011; 4: 161–165.

Colliard C, *et al.* *Strong reproductive barriers in a narrow hybrid zone of West-Mediterranean green toads (Bufo viridis subgroup) with Plio-Pleistocene divergence.* BMC Evolutionary Biology 2008; 10: 232.

Cördük N, *et al.* *Taxonomic status of a newly described island population of the smooth newt Lissotriton vulgaris (Linnaeus, 1758) from Bozcaada (Canakkale, Turkey).* Turkish Journal of Zoology 2017; 41: 189–195.

Cvetkovic D, *et al.* *Bergmann's rule in amphibians. Combining demographic and ecological parameters to explain body size variation among populations in the common toad Bufo bufo.* Journal of Zoological Systematics and Evolutionary Research 2009; 47: 171–180.

Delfino M, Bar-Oz G, Weissbrod L. *Recent shrinkage of the range of the eastern spadefoot toad, Pelobates syriacus (Amphibia: Anura): archaeological evidence from the Bronze Age in Israel.* Zoology in the Middle East 2007; 40: 45–52.

Denoël M. *On the identification of paedomorphic and overwintering larval newts based on cloacal shape: review and guidelines.* Current Zoology 2017; 63: 165–173.

Diaz-Rodriguez J, *et al.* *Molecular*

evidence for cryptic candidate species in Iberian Pelodytes (Anura, Pelodytidae). Molecular Phylogenetics and Evolution 2015; 83: 224–241.

Diaz-Rodriguez J, *et al.* *Integration of molecular, bioacoustical and morphological data reveals two new cryptic species of Pelodytes (Anura, Pelodytidae) from the Iberian Peninsula.* Zootaxa 2017; 4243: 1–41.

Diego-Rasilla FJ, Luengo RM. *Celestial orientation in the marbled newt (Triturus marmoratus).* Journal of Ethology 2002; 20: 137–141.

Disi AM, Böhme W. *Zoogeography of the amphibians and reptiles of Syria, with additional new records.* Herpetozoa 1996; 9: 63–70.

Dubey S, Dufresnes C. *An extinct vertebrate preserved by its living hybridogenetic descendant.* Scientific Reports 2017; 7: 12768.

Dubey S, *et al.* *Herps without borders: a new newt case and a review of transalpine alien introductions in Western Europe.* Amphibia-Reptilia 2018; doi: 10.1163/15685381-20181028.

Dubois A, Raffaëlli J. *A new ergotaxonomy of the family Salamandridae Goldfuss, 1820 (Amphibia, Urodela).* Alytes 2009; 26: 1–85.

Dufresnes C, *et al.* *Stripeless tree frogs (Hyla meridionalis) with stripes on the Canary Islands.* Salamandra 2011; 47: 232–236.

Dufresnes C, Perrin N. *Effect of biogeographic history on population vulnerability in European amphibians.* Conservation Biology 2015; 4: 1235–1241.

Dufresnes C, *et al.* *Inferring the degree of incipient speciation in secondary contact zones of closely related lineages of Palearctic green toads (Bufo viridis subgroup).* Heredity 2014; 113: 9–20.

Dufresnes C, *et al.* *Timeframe of speciation inferred from secondary contact zones in the European tree frog radiation (Hyla arborea group).* BMC Evolutionary Biology 2015; 15: 155.

Dufresnes C, *et al.* *Evolutionary melting pots: a biodiversity hotspot shaped by ring diversifications around the Black Sea in the Eastern tree frog (Hyla orientalis).* Molecular Ecology 2016; 25: 4285–4300.

Dufresnes C, *et al.* *Cryptic invasion of Italian pool frogs (Pelophylax bergeri) across Western Europe unravelled by multilocus phylogeography.* Biological Invasions 2017; 19: 1407–1420.

Dufresnes C, *et al.* *Multiple uprising invasions of Pelophylax water frogs, potentially inducing a new hybridogenetic complex.* Scientific Reports 2017; 7: 6506.

Dufresnes C, *et al.* *Invasion genetics*

of marsh frogs (Pelophylax ridibundus sensu lato) in Switzerland. Biological Journal of the Linnean Society 2018; 123: 402–410.

Dufresnes C, et al. Phylogeography of Aegean green toads (Bufo viridis subgroup): continental hybrid swarm vs. insular diversification with discovery of a new island endemic. BMC Evolutionary Biology 2018; 18: 67.

Dufresnes C, et al. Genomic evidence for cryptic speciation in tree frogs from the Apennine Peninsula, with description of Hyla perrini sp. nov. Frontiers in Ecology and Evolution 2018.

Dufresnes C. Patterns of amphibian diversity in the Western-Palearctic. The Herpetological Bulletin 2018.

Dzukic G, et al. Historical and contemporary ranges of the spadefoot toads Pelobates spp. (Amphibia: Anura) in the Balkan Peninsula. Acta zoological cracoviensia 2005; 48A: 1–9.

Ebrahimi M, Kami HG, Stöck M. First description of egg sacs and early larval development in Hynobiid salamanders (Urodela, Hynobiidae, Batrachuperus) from North-Eastern Iran. Asiatic Herpetological Research 2004; 10: 168–175.

Ebrahimi M, et al. Embryo and larval development of Iranian near eastern brown frogs, Rana macrocnemis pseudodalmatina Eiselt & Schmidtler, 1971 (Amphibia: Ranidae), in Alang Dareh foest, north-eastern Iran. Zoology in the Middle East 2008; 43: 75–84.

Eleftherakos K, Sotiropoulos K, Polymeni RM. Conservation units in the insular endemic salamander Lyciasalamandra helverseni (Urodela, Salamandridae). Annales Zoologici Fennici 2007; 44: 387–399.

Eggert C, et al. The declining spadefoot toad, Pelobates fuscus (Pelobatidae): paleo and recent environmental changes as a major influence on current population structure and status. Conservation Genetics 2006; 7: 185–195.

Escoriza D. Predation of Hyla intermedia egg-clutches by tadpoles of Discoglossus pictus in Sicily. Herpetology Notes 2014; 7: 575–576.

Faraone FP, et al. The large invasive population of Xenopus laevis in Sicily, Italy. Amphibia-Reptilia 2008; 29: 405–412.

Farjallah S, et al. Pattern of genetic diversity of North African green frog Pelophylax saharicus (Amphibia) in Tunisia. Pakistan Journal of Zoology 2012; 44: 901–907.

Ficetola GS, et al. Habitat availability for amphibians and extinction threat: a global analysis. Diversity and Distributions 2005; 21: 302–311.

Fijarczyk A, et al. Nuclear and mitochondrial phylogeography of the European fire-bellied toads Bombina bombina and Bombina variegata supports their independent histories. Molecular Ecology 2011; 20: 3381–3398.

Fisher MC, Garner TWJ. The relationship between the emergence of Batrachochytrium dendrobatidis, the international trade in amphibians and introduced amphibian species. Fungal Biology Reviews 2007; 21: 2–9.

Franzen M. A distribution record of the banded newt, Triturus vittatus, from the Mesopotamian plain, southeastern Turkey. Herpetological Bulletin 2000; 74: 26–28.

Garcia-Porta J, et al. Molecular phylogenetics and historical biogeography of the west-palearctic common toads (Bufo bufo species complex). Molecular Phylogenetics and Evolution 2012; 63: 113–130.

Garner TWJ. Chytrid fungus in Europe. Emerging Infectious Diseases 2005; 11: 1639–1641.

Göçmen B, Arikan H, Yalcinkaya D. A new Lycian salamander, threatened with extinction, from the Göynük Canyon (Antalya, Anatolia), Lyciasalamandra irfani n. sp. (Urodela: Salamandridae). North-Western Journal of Zoology 2011; 7: 151–160.

Göçmen B, Akman B. Lyciasalamandra arikani n. sp. & L. yehudahi n. sp. (Amphibia: Salamandridae), two new Lycian salamanders from Southwestern Anatolia. North-Western Journal of Zoology 2012; 8: 181–194.

Göçmen B, et al. New records of the Turkish Lycian salamanders (Lyciasalamandra, Salamandridae). North-Western Journal of Zoology 2013; 9: 319–328.

Göçmen B, et al. Notes on the reproduction of Lyciasalamandra atifi (Basoglu, 1967) (Amphibia: Salamandridae) from Cebireis Mountain (Antalya, Turkey). Biharean Biologist 2013; 7: 52–53.

Göçmen B, Karis M. Comparative study on the endangered Marmaris Lycian salamander populations, Lyciasalamandra flavimembris (Mutz & Steinfarts, 1995) (Caudata: Salamandridae), with the description of several new localities. North-Western Journal of Zoology 2017; 13: 49–57.

Gomez A, Lunt D. Refugia within refugia: patterns of phylogeographic concordance in the Iberian Peninsula. Pp 155-188 in: Phylogeography of Southern European Refugia, Springer Netherlands; 2017.

Gomez D, et al. The role of nocturnal vision in mate choice: females prefer conspicuous males in the European

tree frog (Hyla arborea). Proceedings of the Royal Society B: Biological Sciences 2009; 276: 2351–5358.

Gonçalves, H, et al. Multilocus phylogeography of the common midwife toad, Alytes obstetricans (Anura, alytidae): Contrasting patterns of lineage diversification and genetic structure in the Iberian refugium. Molecular Phylogenetics and Evolution 2015; 93: 363–379.

Goricki S, et al. Environmental DNA in subterranean biology: range extension and taxonomic implications for Proteus. Scientific Reports 2017; 7: 45054.

Gosner KL. A simplified table for staging anuran embryos and larvae with notes on identification. Herpetologica 1960; 16: 183–190.

Gül S. Habitat preferences of endemic Caucasian parsley frog (Pelodytes caucasicus) Boulenger, 1896 and Caucasian salamander (Mertensiella caucasica) (Waga, 1876) based on bioclimatic data of Fırtına valley (Rize, Northeastern Anatolia). Anadolu Doga Bilimleri Dergisi 2014; 5: 24–29.

Gül S, Kutrup B, Ozdemir N. Patterns of distribution of tree frogs in Turkey based on molecular data. Amphibia-Reptilia 2012; 33: 95–103.

Gutierrez-Rodriguez J, et al. Present and past climatic effects on the current distribution and genetic diversity of the Iberian spadefoot toad (Pelobates cultripes): an integrative approach. Journal of Biogeography 2017; 44: 245–258.

Gvozdik V. Second species of tree frog, Hyla orientalis (formerly H. arborea) from Iran confirmed by acoustic data. Herpetology Notes 2010; 3: 41–44.

Gvozdik V, Moravec J, Kratochvil L. Geographic morphological variation in parapatric Western Palearctic tree frogs, Hyla arborea and Hyla savignyi: are related species similarly affected by climatic conditions? Biological Journal of the Linnean Society 2008; 95: 539–556.

Harris DJ, Batista V, Carretero MA. Diversity of 12S mitochondrial DNA sequences in Iberian and North-west African water frogs across predicted geographic barriers. Herpetozoa 2003; 16: 81–83.

Hauswaldt JS, et al. Hybridization of two ancient salamander lineages: molecular evidence for endemic spectacled salamanders from the Apennine peninsula. Journal of Zoology 2011; 284: 248–256.

Herczeg D, et al. Taxonomic composition and ploidy level among European water frogs (Anura: Ranidae: Pelophylax) in eastern Hungary. Journal of Zoological Systematics and Evolutionary Research 2016; 55: 129–137.

Hernandez A, Escoriza D. *Easternmost record of Salamandra algira splendens in Morocco.* Boletín de la Asociación Herpetológica Española 2017; 28: 60–61.

Hewitt G. *The genetic legacy of the Quaternary ice ages.* Nature 2000; 405: 907–913.

Hewitt G. *Quaternary phylogeography: the roots of hybrid zones.* Genetica 2011; 139: 617–638.

Hödl W, Amezquita A. *Visual signalling in anuran amphibians.* Pp 121-141 in Anuran communication. Smithsonian Inst. Press, Washington 2001.

Holsbeek G, et al. *Genetic detection of multiple exotic water frog species in Belgium illustrates the need for monitoring and immediate action.* Biological Invasions 2010; 12: 1459–1463.

Hoffman EA, Blouin MS. *A review of colour pattern polymorphisms in anurans.* Biological Journal of the Linnean Society 2000; 70: 633–665.

Hoffman F, Kloas W. *Estrogens can disrupt amphibian mating behavior.* PLoS ONE 2012; 7: e32097.

Iannella M, Cerasoli F, Biondi M. *Unravelling climate influences on the distribution of the parapatric newts Lissotriton vulgaris meridionalis and L. italicus.* Frontiers in Zoology 2017; 14: 55.

Jaquiéry J, et al. *Good genes drive female choice for mating partners in the lek-breeding European tree frog.* Evolution 2009; 64: 108–115.

Kalayci TB, Ozdemir N. *New locality records for Turkish endemic species Rana tavasensis (Baran and Atatür, 1986).* Journal of Anatolian Environmental & Animal Sciences 2018; 2: 77–79.

Kalayci TB, Kalayci G, Ozdemir N. *Phylogeny and systematics of Anatolian mountain frogs.* Biochemical Systematics and Ecology 2017; 73: 26–34.

Kami HG, Bashirichelkasari N. *Preliminary study of reproduction in the Talysh toad (Bufo eichwaldi) in northern Iran.* Herpetology Notes 2018; 11: 31–33.

Karis M, Göcmen B, Mermer A. *Taxonomical and biological comparison of two Luschan's Lycian salamander, Lyciasalamandra luschani (Steindachner, 1891) (Urodela: Salamandridae) populations from southwestern Anatolia.* South Western Journal of Horticulture, Biology and Environment 2015; 6: 107–136.

Kaya U. *Advertisement call of the Caucasian Parsley frog, Pelodytes caucasicus Boulenger 1896 (Pelodytidae, Anura) in Turkey.* Israel Journal of Zoology 2002; 48: 263–272.

Kaya U, Cevik IE. *New distributional records for Rana bedriagae caralitana in Anatolia.* Turkish Journal of Zoology 2002; 26: 381–383.

Kidov AA. *Notes on the biology of Iranian long-legged wood frog (Rana macrocnemis pseudodalmatina Eiselt and Schmidtler, 1971) in southeastern Azerbaijan.* Current Herpetology 2010; 10: 109–114.

Köhler J, et al. *The use of bioacoustics in anuran taxonomy: theory, terminology, methods and recommendations for best practice.* Zootaxa 2017; 4251: 1–124.

Kraus F. *Impacts from invasive reptiles and amphibians.* Annual Review of Ecology, Evolution, and Systematics 2015; 46: 75–97.

Kutrup B, Bülbül U. *Comparison of skeletal muscle protein bands and trunk vertebrae count between Ommatotriton ophryticus nesterovi and O. o. ophryticus populations in Turkey.* Turkish Journal of Zoology 2011; 35: 579–584.

Langhelle A, Lindell MJ, Nyström P. *Effects of ultraviolet radiation on amphibian embryonic and larval development.* Journal of Herpetology 1999; 3: 449–456.

Lillo F, et al. *Identification and potential origin of naturalized clawed frogs Xenopus (Anura: Pipidae) in Sicily based on mitochondrial and nuclear DNA.* Italian Journal of Zoology 2013; 80(4): 566–573.

Litvinchuk SN, et al. *Taxonomic status of Triturus vittatus (Amphibia: Salamandridae) in western Turkey: trunk vertebrae count, genome size and allozyme data.* Amphibia-Reptilia 2005; 26: 305–323.

Litvinchuk SN, et al. *A new species of common toads from the Talysh mountains, south-eastern Caucasus: genome size, allozyme, and morphological evidences.* Russian Journal of Herpetology 2008; 15: 19–43.

Litvinchuk SN, et al. *Phylogeographic patterns of genetic diversity in the common spadefoot toad, Pelobates fuscus (Anura: Pelobatidae), reveals evolutionary history, postglacial range expansion and secondary contact.* Organisms Diversity and Evolution 2013; 13: 433–451.

Lymberakis P, et al. *Mitochondrial phylogeography of Rana (Pelophylax) populations in the Eastern Mediterranean region.* Molecular Phylogenetics and Evolution 2017; 44: 115–125.

Maia-Carvalho B, et al. *Multilocus assessment of phylogenetic relationships in Alytes (Anura, Alytidae).* Molecular Phylogenetics and Evolution 2014; 79: 270–278.

Marsh DM, Trenham PC. *Metapopulation dynamics and amphibian conservation.* Conservation Biology 2001; 15: 40–49.

Marsh DM, et al. *Forest roads as partial barriers to terrestrial salamander movement.* Conservation Biology 2005; 19: 2004–2008.

Martinez-Solano I, et al. *Mitochondrial DNA phylogeography of Lissotriton boscai (Caudata, Salamandridae): evidence for old, multiple refugia in an Iberian endemic.* Molecular Ecology 2006; 15: 3375–3388.

Mattoccia M, et al. *Phylogeography of an Italian endemic salamander (genus Salamandrina): glacial refugia, postglacial expansions, and secondary contact.* Biological Journal of the Linnean Society 2011; 104: 903–922.

Matushkina KA, Kidov AA. *Reproduction of Talysh common toad Bufo eichwaldi Litvinchuk, Rosanov, Borkin et Skorinov, 2008 (Amphibia: Anura: Bufonidae) in mountains and foothills of Azerbaijan Talysh.* Bulletin of TSU 2013; 18: 3042–3044.

Matushkina KA, Yanchurevich OV, Kidov AA. *Age and growth of the Eichwald's toad (Bufo eichwaldi Litvinchuk, Borkin, Skorinov et Rosanov, 2008) in the Lenkoran lowland (southeastern Azerbaijan).* Modern Herpetology 2015; 15: 114–119.

Mediani M, Brito JC, Fahd S. *Atlas of the amphibians and reptiles of northern Morocco: updated distribution and patterns of habitat selection.* Basic and Applied Herpetology 2015; 29: 81–107.

Merabet K, et al. *New occurrence record of the Algerian ribbed newt Pleurodeles nebulosus (Guichenot, 1850) in Algeria.* The Herpetological Bulletin 2016; 137: 43.

Modry D, et al. *Amphibians and reptiles of the Hashemite kingdom of Jordan.* Pp 407–420 in Denisia 14 – Zugleich Kataloge der Oberösterreichischen Landesmuseen 2004.

Munwes I, et al. *The change in genetic diversity down the core-edge gradient in the eastern spadefoot toad (Pelobates syriacus).* Molecular Ecology 2010; 19: 2675–2689.

Muths E, et al. *Heterogeneous responses of temperate-zone amphibian populations to climate change complicates conservation planning.* Scientific Reports 2017; 7: 17102.

Najibzadeh M, et al. *Food habits of the endemic long legged wood frog Rana pseudodalmatina in Northern Iran.* Vestnik zoologii 2016; 50: 363–368.

Najibzadeh M, et al. *Molecular phylogenetic relationships among Anatolian-Hyrcanian brown frog taxa*

(Ranidae: Rana). Amphibia-Reptilia 2017; 38: 339–350.

Nicolas V, et al. Phylogeographic patterns in North African water frog Pelophylax saharicus (Anura: Ranidae). Journal of Zoological Systematics and Evolutionary Research 2015; 53: 239–248.

Olgun K, et al. Age, size and growth of the southern crested newt Triturus karelinii (Strauch 1870) in a population from Bozdag (Western Turkey). Amphibia-Reptilia 2005; 26: 223–230.

Olgun K, et al. Range extensions of two salamanders Neurergus strauchii "Stendachnet, 1887) and Salamandra infraimmaculata (Martens, 1885) "Caudata Salamandridae) from Anatolia, Turkey. Russian Journal of Herpetology 2015; 4: 289–296.

Olgun K, et al. A new subspecies of Anatolia newt, Neurergus strauchii "Steindachner, 1887) (Urodela: Salamandridae) from Tunceli, Eastern Turkey. Russian Journal of Herpetology 2016; 23: 271–277.

Oguz MN, Göçmen B, Yalcinkaya D. Comparison of Lyciasalamandra atifi (Basoglu, 1967) (Urodela: Salamadridae) populations with description of three new subspecies from Antalya Province. South Western Journal of Horticulture, Biology and Environment 2016; 7: 61–113.

Ozdemir N, et al. Phylogeny of Neurergus crocatus and Neurergus strauchii in Turkey based on morphological and molecular data. Herpetologica 2009; 65: 280–291.

Pabijan M, et al. The dissection of a Pleistocene refugium: phylogeography of the smooth newt, Lissotriton vulgaris, in the Balkans. Journal of Biogeography 2015; 42: 671–683.

Pabijan M, et al. Isolation and gene flow in a speciation continuum in newts. Molecular Phylogenetics and Evolution 2017; 116: 1–12.

Pagano A, Joly P. Limits of the morphometric method for field identification of water frogs. Alytes 1999; 16: 130–138.

Pagano A, et al. Distribution and habitat use of water frog hybrid complexes in France. Global Ecology and Biogeography 2001; 10: 433–441.

Pagano A, et al. Frog alien species: a way for genetic invasion? Comptes Rendus Biologies 2003; 326.

Pearman PB, Garner TWJ. Susceptibility of Italian agile frog populations to an emerging strain of Ranavirus parallels population genetic diversity. Ecology Letter 2005; 8: 401–408.

Pellet J, Schmidt BR. Monitoring distributions using call surveys: estimating site occupancy, detection probabilities and inferring absence.

Biological Conservation 2005; 123: 27–35.

Perl RGB, et al. Natural history and conservation of the rediscovered Hula painted frog, Latonia nigriventer. Contributions to Zoology 2017; 86: 11–37.

Plötner J, et al. Genetic data reveal that water frogs of Cyprus (genus Pelophylax) are an endemic species of Messinian origin. Zoosystematics and Evolution 2012; 88: 261–283.

Polymeni RM, Radea C, Papanayotou C. Diet composition of the salamander Lyciasalamandra luschani basoglui on the Greek island of Kastellorizo in the southeast Aegean Sea. Asian Herpetological Research 2011; 2: 155–160.

Pramuk, et al. Around the world in 10 million years: biogeography of the nearly cosmopolitan true toads (Anura: Bufonidae). Global Ecology and Biogeography 2017; doi: 10.1111/j.1466-8238.2007.00348.x

Pruvost NBM, Hoffmann A, Reyer HU. Gamete production patterns, ploidy, and population genetics reveal evolutionary significant units in hybrid water frogs (Pelophylax esculentus). Ecology and Evolution 2013; 3: 2933–2946.

Pyron RA, Wiens JJ. A large-scale phylogeny of Amphibia including over 2800 species, and a revised classification of extant frogs, salamanders, and caecilians. Molecular Phylogenetics and Evolution 2011; 61: 543–583.

Radojicic JM, et al. Extensive mitochondrial heteroplasmy in hybrid water frog (Pelophylax spp.) populations from southeast Europe. Ecology and Evolution 2015; 5: 4529–4541.

Rafinska A. Reproductive biology of the fire-bellied toads, Bombina bombina and B. variegata (Anura: Discoglossidae): egg size, clutch site and larval period length differences. Biological Journal of the Linnean Society 1991; 43: 197–210.

Recuero E, et al. Mitochondrial differentiation and biogeography of Hyla meridionalis (Anura: Hylidae): an unusual phylogeographical pattern. Journal of Biogeography 2007; 34: 1207–1219.

Recuero E, Garcia-Paris M. Evolutionary history of Lissotriton helveticus. Bayesian assessment of ancestral vs. recent colonization of the Iberian Peninsula. Molecular Phylogenetics and Evolution 2011; 60: 170–182.

Recuero E, et al. Multilocus species tree analyses resolve the radiation of the widespread Bufo bufo species group (Anura, Bufonidae). Molecular Phylogenetics and Evolution 2012;

62: 71–86.

Recuero E, et al. Evolutionary history of Ichthyosaura alpestris (Caudata, Salamandridae) inferred from the combined analysis of nuclear and mitochondrial markers. Molecular Phylogenetics and Evolution 2014; 81: 207–220.

Riberon A, et al. Phylogeography of the Alpine salamander, Salamandra atra (Salamandridae) and the influence of the Pleistocene climatic oscillations on population divergence. Molecular Ecology 2001; 10: 2555–2560.

Rodriguez A, et al. Inferring the shallow phylogeny of true salamanders (Salamandra) by multiple phylogenomic approaches. Molecular Phylogenetics and Evolution 2017; 115: 16–26.

Romanazzi E, Bonato L. Updating the range of the narrowly distributed endemites Salamandra atra aurorae and S. atra pasubiensis. Amphibia-Reptilia 2014; 35: 123–128.

Romano A, et al. Distribution and morphological characterization of the endemic Italian salamanders Salamandrina perspicillata (Savi, 1821) and S. terdigitata (Bonnaterre, 1789) (Caudata: Salamandridae). Italian Journal of Zoology 2009; 76: 422–432.

Rowe G, Harris DJ, Beebee TJC. Lusitania revisited: a phylogeographic analysis of the natterjack toad Bufo calamita across its entire biogeographical range. Molecular Phylogenetics and Evolution 2006; 39: 335–346.

Santucci F, Nascetti G, Bullini L. Hybrid zones between two genetically differentiated forms of the pond frog Rana lessonae in southern Italy. Journal of Evolutionary Biology 1996; 9: 429–450.

Schmidtler JJ, Schmidtler JF. Untersuchungen an westpersischen Berbachmolchen der Gattung Neurergus (Caudata, Salamandrinae). Salamandra 1975; 11: 84–98.

Schneider C, Schneider W. The Kurdistan newts of the Genus Neurergus in Iraq (Caudata: Salamandridae). Herpetozoa 2011; 23: 3–20.

Sillero N, et al. Updated distribution and biogeography of amphibians and reptiles of Europe. Amphibia-Reptilia 2014; 35: 1–31.

Skorinov DV, et al. Two new cases of paedomorphosis in the Caucasian newts: Ommatotriton ophryticus (the first record) and Lissotriton vulgaris lantzi. Russian Journal of Herpetology 2009; 16: 16–18.

Skorinov DV, et al. Distribution and conservation status of the Caucasian newt, Lissotriton lantzi

(Wolterstorff, 1914). Russian Journal of Herpetology 2014; 21: 251–268.

Sotiropoulos K, et al. *Phylogeny and biogeography of the alpine newt* Mesotriton alpestris *(Salamandridae, Caudata), inferred from mtDNA sequences.* Molecular Phylogenetics and Evolution 2007; 45: 211–226.

Sos T, Hegyeli Z. *Characteristic morphotype distribution predicts the extended range of the "Transylvanian" smooth newt,* Lissotriton vulgaris ampelensis *(Fuhn, 1951), in Romania.* North-Western Journal of Zoology 2014; 11: 34–40.

Steinwarz D, Schneider H. *Distribution and bioacoustics of* Rana perezi *Seoane, 1885 (Amphibia, Anura, Ranidae) in Tunisia.* Bonner zoologische Beiträge 1991; 42: 283–297.

Stöck M, et al. *Post-Messinian evolutionary relationships across the Sicilian channel: Mitochondrial and nuclear markers link a new green toad from Sicily to African relatives.* BMC Evolutionary Biology 2008; 8: 56.

Szabolcs M, Mizsei E. *First record of the eastern spadefoot toad (*Pelobates syriacus *Boettger, 1889) in Albania.* North-Western Journal of Zoology 2017; 13: 175–176.

Tarkhnisnvili DN, Serbinova IA. *The ecology of the Caucasian salamander (*Mertensiella caucasica *Waga) in a local population.* Asiatic Herpetological Research 1993; 5: 147–165.

Tarkhnisnvili DN, Hille A, Böhme W. *Humid forest refugia, speciation and secondary introgression between evolutionary lineages: differentiation in a Near Eastern brown frog,* Rana macrocnemis. Biological Journal of the Linnean Society 2001; 74: 141–156.

Tessa G, Crottini A, Andreone F. *A new finding of* Salamandra lanzai *in Upper Sangone Valley (NW Italy) marks the species' most disjunct population (Amphibia: Urodela: Salamandridae).* Acta Herpetologica 2007; 2: 53–58.

Tok CV, et al. *A new subspecies,* Lyciasalamandra atigi oezi *n. ssp. (Urodela: Salamandridae) from Gazipasa (Antalya, Turkey).* Ecologica Montenegrina 2016; 9: 38–45.

Tosunoglu M, Taskavak E. *A preliminary study on morphology and serology of* Pelodytes caucasicus *Boulenger 1896 populations from north-eastern Turkey.* Pakistan Journal of Biological Sciences 2004; 7: 1186–1190.

Tosunoglu M, Ayaz D, Göcmen B. *On specimens of* Rana ridibunda *Pallas 1771 (Anura: Ranidae) collected from Yagmapinar (Karapinar-Konya).* Anadolu University Journal of Science and Technology 2005; 6: 55–59.

Uzum N, et al. *Body size and age structure of a breeding population portion of the Urmia salamander,* Neurergus crocatus *Cope, 1862 (Caudata: Salamandridae).* Italian Journal of Zoology 2011; 78: 209–214.

van der Meijden A, et al. *Phylogenetic relationships of Sardinian cave salamanders, genus* Hydromantes, *based on mitochondrial and nuclear DNA sequence data.* Molecular Phylogenetics and Evolution 2009; 51: 399–404.

van Riemsdijk I, et al. *The Near East as a cradle of biodiversity: a phylogeography of banded newts (genus* Ommatotriton*) reveals extensive inter- and intraspecific genetic differentiation.* Molecular Phylogenetics and Evolution 2017; 114: 73–81.

Veith M, Steinfarz S. *When non-monophyly results in taxonomic consequences – the case of* Mertensiella *within the* Salamandridae *(Amphibia: Urodela).* Salamandra 2004; 40: 67–80.

Veith M, Kosuch J, Vences M. *Climatic oscillations triggered post-Messinian speciation of Western Palearctic brown frogs (Amphibia, Ranidae).* Molecular Phylogenetics and Evolution 2003; 26: 310–327.

Veith M, et al. *Palaeoclimatic changes explain Anatolian mountain frog evolution: a test for alternating vicariance and dispersal events.* Molecular Ecology 2003; 12: 185–199.

Veith M, et al. *Historical biogeography of Western Palaearctic pelobatid and pelodytid frogs: a molecular phylogenetic perspective.* Contributions to Zoology 2006; 75: 109–120.

Veith M, et al. *Seven at one blow: the origin of major lineages of the viviparous Lycian salamanders (*Lyciasalamandra *Veith and Steinfartz, 2004) was triggered by a single paleo-historic event.* Amphibia-Reptilia 2016; 37: 373–387.

Vences M, et al. *Field body temperatures and heating rates in a montane frog population. The importance of black dorsal pattern for thermoregulation.* Annales Zoologici Fennici 2002; 39: 209–220.

Vences M, et al. *Radically different phylogeographies and patterns of genetic variation in two European brown frogs, genus* Rana. Molecular Phylogenetics and Evolution 2013; 68: 657–670.

Vences M, et al. *New insights on phylogeography and distribution of painted frogs (*Discoglossus*) in northern Africa and the Iberian Peninsula.* Amphibia-Reptilia 2014; 35: 305–320.

Vences M, et al. *Diversity and distribution of deep mitochondrial lineages of the common frog,* Rana temporaria, *in northern Spain.* Salamandra 2017; 53: 25–33.

Vörös J, et al. *Surveying Europe's only cave-dwelling chordate species (*Proteus anguinus*) using environmental DNA.* PLoS ONE 2017; 12: e0170945.

Vucić M, et al. *Molecular identification of species and hybrids of water frogs (genus* Pelophylax*) from Lake Skadar, Southeast Adriatic drainages (Amphibia: Ranidae).* Salamandra 2018; 54: 147–157.

Vukov TD, et al. *Morphometrics of the yellow-bellied toad (*Bombina variegata*) in the Central Balkans: Implications for taxonomy and zoogeography.* Zoological Studies 2006; 45: 213–222.

Wielstra B, Arntzen JW. *Description of a new species of crested newt, previously subsumed in* Triturus ivanbureschi *(Amphibia: Caudata: Salamandridae).* Zootaxa 2016; 4109: 73–80.

Wielstra B, Baird AB, Arntzen JW. *A multimarker phylogeography of crested newts (*Triturus cristatus *superspecies) reveals cryptic species.* Molecular Phylogenetics and Evolution 2013; 67: 167–175.

Wielstra B, et al. *Tracing glacial refugia of* Triturus *newts based on mitochondrial DNA phylogeography and species distribution modelling.* Frontiers in Zoology 2013; 10: 13.

Wielstra B, Bozkurt E, Olgun K. *The distribution and taxonomy of* Lissotriton *newts in Turkey (Amphibia, Salamandridae).* ZooKeys 2015; 484: 11–23.

Williams RN, et al. *Amphibian malformations and inbreeding.* Biology Letters 2008; 4: 549–552.

Yuan ZY, et al. *Spatiotemporal diversification of the true frogs (Genus* Rana*): A historical framework for a widely studied group of model organisms.* Systematic Biology 2016; 65: 824–842.

Zhang P, et al. *Phylogeny and biogeography of the family* Salamandridae *(Amphibia: Caudata) inferred from complete mitochondrial genomes.* Molecular Phylogenetics and Evolution 2008; 49: 586–597.

Zivari S, Kami HG. *Skeletochronological assessment of age in the Persian mountain salamander,* Paradactylodon gorganensis *(Clergue-Gazeau and Thorn, 1979) (Caudata: Hynobiidae) from Golestan Province, Iran.* Caspian Journal of Environmental Science 2017; 15: 75–84.

Index of Scientific Names

Index of Common Names